FIFTY - SEVEN

FIFTY - SEVEN

*SOME ACCOUNT OF THE
ADMINISTRATION OF INDIAN DISTRICTS DURING
THE REVOLT OF THE BENGAL ARMY.*

HENRY GEORGE KEENE, C.I.E., M.R.A.S.

GYAN

Published by

Gyan Publishing House
5, Ansari Road
Daryaganj, New Delhi-110002
Phone: 011-47034999, 9811692060
E-mail: books@gyanbooks.com

Distribution Network
gyanbooks.com
India, USA, Canada, UK, Australia, France

ISBN: 978-81-212-8722-7 (PB)
First Published, 1883

2nd Impression 2023

Printed at: Gyan Press, Delhi.

FIFTY - SEVEN
AUTHOR: HENRY GEORGE KEENE

FIFTY-SEVEN.

SOME ACCOUNT OF THE ADMINISTRATION OF INDIAN DISTRICTS DURING THE REVOLT OF THE BENGAL ARMY.

BY

HENRY GEORGE KEENE, C.I.E., M.R.A.S.,

AUTHOR OF "THE FALL OF THE MUGHAL EMPIRE," ETC., ETC.

LONDON:
W. H. ALLEN & CO., 13 WATERLOO PLACE. S.W.

1883.

Dedication.

TO MY COMRADES OF THE MUTINY-TIME;
IN AFFECTIONATE REGARD FOR
THE SURVIVORS,
AND IN LOVING MEMORY OF
THOSE WHO ARE NO MORE;
THESE IMPERFECT RECORDS OF THEIR SERVICES ARE
INSCRIBED.

[The materials of the following pages will be chiefly found in the official "Narratives," furnished to the Government of the North-Western Provinces by Collectors and Commissioners at the time. I have not referred to the Dehli Division which then formed a part of those Provinces. The reason is that the Civil rule was entirely overthrown, for the moment, in that Division, where the events fell under the control of the Military authorities. Many of the Civil officers fell at their posts; including Simon Fraser the Commissioner, killed at the gate of the Palace, and the gallant John Wedderburn, Magistrate of Hissar, who refused to leave his District, and was murdered on his way home from office. Some details are given from recollection. Names of well-known places have been written according to English usage. In regard to others, the modern system of transliteration adopted by the Indian Government has been observed.]

PREFACE.

These pages are not offered as a history of the Sepoy Mutiny and consequent War, which have been exhaustively related by professional writers. But there were special services performed in many different parts of India, and most of all in the country between the Satlaj and the Karmnása, which were necessary, not only to the utilisation of the deeds of the soldier, but even to their very doing. An army could not take the field without due carriage, nor march without supplies and information. Leaders of troops could not tell in what direction to strike, or where to hold their hands, unless accompanied or inspired by just and resolute companions possessed of local knowledge and local influence. In many instances there were, at times, no military agents at all, either troops or leaders; and then the local officers had to raise and command their own levies. Last, and certainly not least, must be remembered the urgent necessity of collecting the revenue.

It was the business of such officers, again, when the war-tide had finally ebbed, to replace the ancient landmarks, and turn the swords into plough-shares and reaping-hooks.

Some account of the manner in which this was done is now, for the first time, offered. Two lessons, at least, may be drawn from the record. One is that, whatever posts are hereafter to be made available to Asiatics,* there is one which – save in the most peaceful and orderly of neighbourhoods, perhaps—should always be reserved to men of European birth and training: I mean, of course, that of District-officer. It is sufficient to reflect what might have been the consequences had districts like Sahāranpur, Meerut, or Etáwa been in the hands of Asiatics during the time that is here treated of. With the greatest loyalty and good-will, Asiatic officers would be always likely to fall into one of two temptations. Either they would show weakness or they would act with undue severity. Nothing but the combination of impartial humanity with an unimpressionable firmness could possibly have nerved Spankie, Dunlop, Hume, and their contemporary District-officers, with the will and power to make head against all the troubles of their position, and to restore order and confidence at the earliest available moment.

---

* "They are specially fit for judicial functions, much more so than for executive or administrative functions."—Lord Hartington in the House of Commons, 23rd August 1883.

The careers of de Boigne, Thomas, Perron, and other adventurers of the last century—no less than that of Avitabîle under Ranjit Singh—show how much this truth was appreciated even by the comparatively uncivilised rulers to whom India was subject then. And it would be a deplorable error if this lesson were to be ignored or neglected now by a Government which, in a much greater degree, has undertaken to regenerate a region so long demoralised by anarchy as Hindustan. If the native powers had to employ European administrators, how much more must Britain!

The other lesson to be heedfully appropriated is the necessity of a just and discriminate use of native talent and loyalty. In most, if not all, of the districts here observed, it will be clear that the exertions of the British District-officers and their European associates —heroic, as we need not hesitate to call them—were only rendered effective by the co-operation of Asiatics, military and civil. If the assistance of Sindhia and Holkar, of Jang Bahádur and the various minor chiefs of the province of Hindustan (to say nothing of the Sikh chiefs to the north and Salár Jang in the Deccan) deserve credit, as they undoubtedly do, no less acknowledgment is due to the fidelity of the Sikhs and Gurkhas, of Hindu clans in one part and (to a less degree) of Muhamadan gentlemen in another; most of all, perhaps, to the exceptional loyalty of bodies of native troops who, amid all temptations, remained "true to their salt," protecting when possible their officers and their officers' families, and following white leaders whom they trusted in the punishment of offenders of their own blood and religion. Nor ought we to forget the faithful among the "Amlah," or subordinate native officials: a class who had much to tempt them from the British cause, and little reason, perhaps, to love it but what they might find in hard work, bad pay, and precarious promotion; even precarious tenure of office. Many of these men did good work.

It is my earnest hope that something has been here set down to give emphasis to both the above-stated doctrines. If India is ever to be made prosperous and happy, it must be by a combination of native merit with European direction and control. The subject races of Her Majesty's Eastern Empire are endowed with many good qualities; but, owing to the long centuries of misrule and anarchy that—with the one brief exception of Akbar and his immediate successors—have crushed their energies, these qualities are mostly of the negative kind. To abstain from drunkenness, from disorder, from debauchery, are hardly felt as difficulties by the masses of the rural population, since they and their fathers have, for some generations, had little scope or opportunity for the practice of those vices. They have still to be taught to acquire secondary wants; to improve their agriculture and commerce; to respect themselves and others; to join in the application of their industry and dexterity for the welfare of the community at large. How far they were from having learned these lessons in 1857–8 is shown by the glimpses of anarchy and civil strife that are obtained in the course of our narrative; and it would be bold to assert that the rural population had come much nearer to the qualifications for Home-Rule in the quarter of a century that has since elapsed. To illustrate and impart these lessons is among the true arts of European civilisation, in spite of its many excesses and defects; and thus we may borrow the words of Virgil to Rome, and say to our country—

"Hæ tibi erunt artes."

If there be any other moral deducible from my story, it is surely this: that it is perilous to keep any class of the population in ignorance. If the sepoys had understood the merest rudiments of contemporary history, they would have known that the British could have no wish to convert them to Christianity, either by force or by fraud. If the Jats and Gujars, and other tribes of the peasantry, who availed themselves of the temporary paralysis of power in Upper India, caused by the mutiny of the Bengal army, had been at all educated, they would have known that England had other soldiers who would soon appear on the scene, and that such outbreaks as theirs must, in any case, end badly for themselves. The agitation of educated men takes a different form, and meets with a different result. However disagreeable may be some of the features of political agitation, it may lead to good when addressed to hearers capable of understanding their evils and how to obtain permanent relief. But the history of all ignorant rural risings shows that, without general instruction, and something which is best represented by a free press, no political progress is possible. These efforts of brute force only lead in the direction of chaos.

H. G. K.

ATHENÆUM,
October, 1883.

CONTENTS.

INDIAN DISTRICTS DURING THE REVOLT.

INTRODUCTORY.

More than a quarter of a century has passed away since the power of Britain in the far East was shaken to its base. The great Native Army that had been formed by Clive in Bengal a hundred years before, and which, in combination with a small contingent of white troops, had carried the banner of England to Prome on one side and to Peshâwar on another, had yielded to Prætorian pride, and had risen against its leaders and its employers in a murderous revolt. The titular "King of Dehli" had been drawn in as a nominal head, and held faded state among a turbulent host of pretended followers in the ruinous halls of his ancestors, the Mughal Emperors of Hindustan. The minor potentates looked on in anxious wonder, or gave a more or less effective support to their foreign allies, of whose ultimate triumph most of them had wisdom enough to entertain forebodings. Among the people there was much confusion; the criminal and lawless benefited by the weakness of the restraining power; the peaceable masses cowered in alarm, and provided as best they could for their own safety. In the words of an impartial observer, a month after the outbreak—

> The situation might be summed up as follows:—Direct communication between Calcutta, Dehli, and the Panjáb was completely interrupted, and the army before Dehli, little over 4,000 strong, was scarcely able to maintain its position. Its base of operations was the Panjáb by the line of Ludiána. Sir J. Lawrence, with heroic devotion, despatched his European regiments to Dehli, but it was doubtful whether the besieging force would be able to remain before the city till their arrival.*

It was in this situation that the qualities and the resources of each isolated representative of British power in Upper India were taxed and strained for a period, the end of which none of them could foresee. Some of these, not unnaturally, succumbed to the appalling problem of maintaining law and order, and protecting life and property, with untrustworthy instruments and against dangers of which no one knew the extent, but no one could possibly over-estimate the magnitude. It is a fact that in no such instance was peace preserved for a moment after they left their stations. By far the majority, however, chose the better part, though they paid dearly for their devotion. As was remarked at the time by a civil officer who gave a splendid example of energy and daring in the administration of his own district,—

> The civilians (superior civil officers) of this Presidency have suffered more severely than any other class of men in the country. There were, when the mutiny commenced, 153 present, about one-third of whom have been killed or wounded. Twenty-nine have been murdered, killed in action, or died of wounds; three died from cholera, or exposure on service, and several have been wounded . . . the Gazettes take no notice of civilians' wounds.—[*The Khakee Risullah*, &c. By R. Wallace Dunlop, C.B. R. Bentley, 1858.]

Nevertheless, these sufferings were not without fruit. Many of the districts were successfully defended and held by these extemporised leaders, whose ordinary professional duties did not go beyond holding trials, presiding at local boards, and the sort of work performed in England by the squires and parsons. M. de Valbezen, an impartial critic, calls attention to these "modest" services of the civilians (official and non-official it should be added), and gives deserved prominence to the defence of the

* *India and the English.* By E. de Valbezen. Allen & Co., 1883.

house at Arrah, though he unhappily deprives the magistrate, Mr. Hereward Wake, C.B., of his due credit by styling him "Mr. Walker." In truth, these "magistrates" (taking the word in its Anglo-Indian sense, denoting the Prefects of Districts), for the most, had to work as military officers, and often as officers without men. Their staff consisted, for the most part, of their official assistants and a few planters—some, like Venables and Dunn, men of great resolution and energy. But of the rank and file little was to be expected. A few sepoys, of doubtful fidelity unless they were Sikhs or Gurkhas; a half-disciplined jail-guard, often in sympathy with the convicts in their charge; a handful of messengers, often faithful fellows, but with no discipline at all: such was the material with which the fiercest passions of thousands were to be stayed, and the occasional raids of disciplined mutineers to be encountered, on pain of loss of life and honour, and of disaster and disgrace to the State.

CHAPTER I.

SAHARANPUR AND MUZAFARNAGAR.

Foremost among the districts thus held must be named Sahāranpur. In the order of districts taken geographically, it comes first, beginning from the northern limit to which the insurrection spread. It stands, moreover, first in two other respects. It formed the bulwark of the hill stations of Mussoorie and Landour, where was then assembled the largest white population north of Calcutta. And it was, in the whole Province, the district in which the defensive attitude of the civil power met with the most uninterrupted and untarnished success. A word about the hill stations and the geographic and social situation of Sahāranpur may, therefore, be not unwelcome.

Sahāranpur is the official title of a "district," or shire, containing 2,219 square miles, with a population of, say, 890,000, about one-third being Musalmáns and the remainder Hindus by creed, though nearly 10 per cent. belong to the Gujar tribe. This is a people of unknown origin who have embraced Hinduism, though they do not reckon among the descendants of the Aryan settlers of Upper India. The district is bounded on the north by the low range of the Siwáliks, on the east by the Ganges, on the south by an imaginary line of demarcation, on the west by the Jumna. It thus stands at the head of the *Duab*, or interamnial country, being on one side adjacent to Rohilkhand, on another to the protected hill state of Náhan, and to other dependencies of the Panjáb. It derives its name from a Muhamadan saint of the famous order of Chist, Sháh Háran by name, who founded the chief town about 1340 A.D., and whose shrine is still an object of veneration to the Muslim community. Lying on one of the lines of march from Central Asia to Dehli and Hindustán, this tract has been for centuries subject to Musalmán influence, many Pathán and Mughal adventurers settling there from time to time, and doing their best to proselytise among the inhabitants. The Emperors, too, resorted to the northern part of the district during the palmy days of the Mughal empire. This is attested to this day by the existence of places called Nurnagar (after Nur Mahl, the wife of Jahángir), and Bádsha Mahl (where are to be seen the ruins of a hunting-lodge, built by Shahjahan, near the head-waters of the canal which he caused to be taken from the Jumna). About the date of Aurangzeb's death the Sikhs invaded it in the pursuance of their first audacious rising. They were for the time expelled and punished; and Musalmán influence revived, though under chiefs more or less practically independent. After the death of Ghulám Kadir—the oppressor of the Emperor Sháh Alam, whom he blinded in 1788—the Sikhs over-ran the country once more, but were expelled by the Mahrattas, who, with French aid, were becoming as powerful in Upper India as they had long been in the Deccan. After Lake had occupied Dehli in 1803, both Sikhs and Mahrattas became engaged with the British, who gradually, however, settled the district in spite of their resistance. Gujar outbreaks occurred in 1813 and 1824, and then the anarchic elements assumed a temporary calm.

Such was the state of Saháranpur in the opening of 1857. The population of the chief town was nearly 50,000, of whom more than half were Muhamadans. The rural tracts contained a population of whom those over thirty years of age had seen anarchy and insurrection, or had heard of it from eye-witnesses. The Rájputs who had been converted to Islám were in sympathy with the King of Dehli and the Crescent generally; the pure

Muslims by descent sighed over the lost grandeur of their race; the Gujars longed to resume the predatory habits of the past; the rest of the Hindus, timid and apathetic, did not care what happened so long as they kept their possessions, real and personal. There were hardly any influential aristocrats to lend help to authority, the long anarchy of bye-gone years having ruined them, as the barons of England were ruined by the Wars of the Roses. Of the 1,916 estates which composed the Domesday-book of the district, the average rental was no more than £20 a year, of which half went to Government and half was the land-holder's income. Surely a social fabric with but little promise of reserve force, whether to resist famine or sustain civil war.

On the eastern side of the district, where the great British Canal leaves the Ganges at Hardwár, there were several places of importance. Hardwár itself is the centre of a group of holy places, visited by millions of Hindu pilgrims year by year. A few miles lower down stands Rurki, the head-quarters of the sapper corps of the Bengal army, the seat of a college of civil engineering, and the scene of a factory known as the Ganges canal workshops. At the time of the outbreak Rurki contained some officers of the Bengal Engineers attached to the canal, the College, and the Sappers, a few conductors and sergeants, and some clerks. There were also a few students residing at the College—say ninety Christians in all, some of them inured to military discipline.

Further north, beyond the Siwálik range, was the picturesque valley of Dehra Dun, lying at the foot of what in military parlance were called "the hills north of Dehra." Many authorities, named in General Newall's recent book,* have dwelt upon the value of garrisons in mountain-retirement, where they could be trained in a temperate climate, and hurled upon the plains in case of emergency. The advice has never been acted on by the Anglo-Indian Government; though there were not

* *The Highlands of India.* By D. Newall, Major-General. Harrison & Co., 1888.

wanting during the troubles of 1857 illustrations of its value. The "hills" were rather a source of anxiety than of aid.

The Dun is a sort of annexe to Sahàranpur, to which it was at one time in administrative subordination. Long since separated into an independent jurisdiction, it possesses some features of singular interest. Lying between the Himalayas and the Siwáliks, it abounds in forest, ravine, and swamp; though the population (including the mountain tracts of Jaunsár and Báwar) hardly reaches 150,000. But a good deal of tea is grown in the valley; the head-quarters of the Trigonometrical Survey of India are there; and it forms the approach to the important European stations of Landour and Mussooree. The former of these is only the military cantonment of the latter, and contains accommodation for about 200 sick and convalescent soldiers from the regiments in the neighbouring plain-stations. Taken together, the united town, scattered over a wide extent of cliffs and ridges, contains schools and convents, hotels and boarding-houses, a club-house and numerous "bungalows," and contains, in the summer, a white population, which has been estimated to average 8,000 souls—mostly women and children. Here, at an elevation of between 7,000 and 8,000 feet above the level of the sea, the wives and families of the officers, who were doing their duty on the reeking plains below, sought escape from the Indian climate, or a restoration of broken and lost strength in a temperature resembling that of the south of France. They were dependent for their food upon supplies brought to them from below; no private banks provided for their financial convenience; but the Government kept up a treasury and public offices at Dehra, the chief town of the valley at the foot of the hills.

The chief upon whom the news of the outbreak threw the duty of providing for and protecting all these varied interests of peace, and controlling the concomitant elements of war, was Mr. Robert Spankie, afterwards better known as a puisne judge of the High Court of Allahabad. A son of Serjeant Spankie, at one time Advocate-General of Bengal, he had been educated at Eton and

Haileybury, and had served about thirteen years in India. The first alarm was given by Colonel R. Baird Smith (afterwards Companion of the Bath and Master of the Calcutta Mint), who was at that time Director-General of the various works of the canals, and had his post at Rurki. The Ganges canal is not only an irrigating stream, its great bulk enables it—with the help of occasional locks—to serve the purposes of navigation. Early in the year certain Hindu contractors had entered into arrangements for supplying some of the down-country cantonments with flour. They brought the grain to the mills at Rurki, where it was ground by water-power; and then sent the flour to Cawnpore and elsewhere by boat. On the 24th April 1857, before any mutiny had occurred, it was brought to Colonel Smith's notice that, while these deliveries were still going on, a rumour had suddenly found currency among the native troops that the agents of Government had mixed bone-dust with the flour. One must know the superstition and almost infantile credulity of the sepoy to understand the full malice of this suggestion. The troops refused to receive the flour, and Colonel Smith reported the affair to the proper authorities. But, standing by itself, the warning was not thought significant.

On the 12th May unmistakable tidings reached Mr. Spankie. Meerut was given over to fire and sword, and the native troops of the garrison had made good their way to Dehli. Next day he sent the Christian women and children to the hills, and prepared for the storm. One of the officers then present had stated since (in a private letter) that the feeling of the European community was at first one of disbelief in anything but a temporary outbreak that would soon be suppressed. Mr. Spankie took another and a truer view of the situation. The Christian population was as follows:—the judge; Mr. Spankie and two or three assistants of the "Covenanted Civil Service"; some clerks, white and coloured; Captain MacDougall and Veterinary-Surgeon Henderson, of the Stud, with their clerks; Lieutenants Brownlow*

* Since Colonel H. Brownlow, R.E., Secretary to Government N.W.P.

and Home of the Engineers. No time was lost in raising men to serve under this staff. For the station itself fifty horse constables, and as many foot; for the city a hundred officers and men; a due proportion of police for the outlying circles being also added to the normal strength of the force. Of Government troops there was a weak company in charge of the district treasury. These men were under a native officer, and had been detached from the 29th Native Infantry, quartered at Moradabad, beyond the river Ganges. The sepoys were probably not regarded with much confidence; the Christians took arms, and collected at Mr. Spankie's house, about a mile from the treasury.

One of the first symptoms that the news of the Mutiny had fallen like a spark on the combustible anarchical material of the district, was that the Gujars and other lawless classes began to gather in large and tumultuary masses, and commit excesses which they well knew would not be permitted for a day in ordinary times. Old scores were paid off; village bankers and quiet landholders were plundered or put under requisition; the papers and accounts of the money-lenders were sought for, and written obligations cancelled by very summary liquidation in fire or water. Unrestrained in this private enterprise, the turbulent classes next turned their attention to the treasuries and record-rooms of outlying offices. Expeditions were at once organised, and the sepoys of the 29th found, for the time, an occupation which served to distract their thoughts from mutinous design. Partly to furnish them with such occupation, and also in order to assert authority and maintain the order whose appointed guardian he was, Mr. Spankie organised several expeditions against the predatory tribes, and was everywhere successful. Villages were visited, and—on special signs of refractoriness—set on fire; many offenders were arrested, defaulting revenue-payers were brought to book. The state of things in the chief town, however, soon became so alarming that Mr. Spankie received orders from divisional head-quarters that he was not to leave it. On the 30th May he led the last expedition in which he took part: and it was well that this was so. Captain MacDougall, of the Stud, was informed, by natives on whom he could rely, that there were elements of mischief in the city that were ready to explode if Mr. Spankie did not remain permanently on the spot. The delay in dealing with Dehli, however justified by military considerations, gave natural encouragement to the disaffected among the Musalman population. Not that they were unanimous. Some of their natural leaders attempted to keep them tranquil, if not loyal. But the head of the city police, who was of that faith, was led astray either by fanaticism or by ambition. He began corresponding with the rebel cabinet at Dehli, and received a patent creating him Nawáb—Lieutenant-Governor—of the Upper Duáb. Mr. Spankie felt that the time had come when, if he was to hold the district properly, he "must have help from without." On his application to the Panjáb authorities, Mr. W. C. Plowden* crossed the Jumna with a party of the 4th Bengal Cavalry under Captain Wyld, and a company of the 5th Native Infantry under Captain Garstin. An immediate check was given to religious enthusiasm of the felonious kind; and the wealthier Hindu bankers and traders strengthened their bolts and bars and slept secure. The "Nawáb" policeman continued to intrigue subterraneously, but he was openly doing his duty. Evidence was not forthcoming, and Mr. Spankie patiently allowed him all possible rope.

On the evening of the 2nd June a crisis took place. Several of the men belonging to the new infantry reinforcement had shown signs of wavering fidelity, and were allowed to take their discharge. They were encamped in the beautiful grounds of the magistrate's house; and while Captain Garstin was sitting at a table preparing to pay them up, they got hold of their arms and fell back upon the gateway of the entrance drive. Mr. Spankie came up, and with nothing but a walking-stick tried to disarm a sepoy who was making ready to fire at him. A native sergeant

* Lately in charge of the Imperial Census.

intervened, and the man was shot. Three officers returning from a drive were at the same time fired upon. Spankie's little hill-messenger ran down from the house with his master's pistol; Wyld called out his men, being shot at thrice while so doing. The mutineers, on this unlooked-for resistance, lost heart, and escaped to their sympathisers in the city in the quickly growing darkness.

Next day arrived Major Bagot with the 3rd Gurkhas or Nasiri Battalion. Their behaviour at Simla had not been free from reproach, and had led the Deputy-Commissioner, Lord William Hay,* to order them away. They came to Sahâranpur, bringing cholera with them. At the same time Mr. Spankie got information that shook his confidence in the rest of Garstin's men and in Wyld's troopers; he also got news that the 29th (a detachment of which furnished his treasury-guard) had mutinied at Moradabad. The Gujars, doubtless egged on by the treacherous "Nawâb," threatened to plunder the treasury.

While the defenders of the central station were exposed to these anxieties, the occupants of Rurki had gone through their share of trouble. But, as the doings there were rather military than civil, they may be here briefly disposed of by the remarks that follow. Some of the Sappers were sent away on duty, some mutinied and deserted, a few remained faithful. Colonel Baird Smith made a rough fortification round the workshops, cast guns, supplied the fire-locks and ammunition of the disarmed Sappers to the Christian garrison, rescued two prisoners from the Rohilkhand rebels, collected a certain amount of revenue from the surrounding estates, and approved himself in all things a worthy helper of the district officer until he was summoned to a more important scene.†

* Now Marquess of Tweeddale, whose services in pacifying the regiment were at the moment the means of saving Simla, and ultimately of enabling them to do indispensable work elsewhere, and so, indirectly, of saving Mussooree also. These services were never duly acknowledged.

† As Engineer-in-Chief with Sir A. Wilson's force, he bore a most influential part in the taking of Dehli in the middle of September. (*Vide* Malleson's *Mutiny*, vol. ii. pp. 3, 4.)

In the Dun, in the meantime, another kind of trouble had arisen. The "lines" of the 1st Gurkhas, who had marched to Dehli, were occupied by the families of the soldiers, guarded by a detachment of eighty men of the regiment under a native officer. The Superintendent blocked the passes by which bad characters might invade the valley without using the high road; this was done by laying down *abattis* of stone and timber, and by enrolling a sort of militia-guard of trustworthy villagers. In the town of Dehra a patrol of the Christians was organised, so that two of them by roster went round the town and environs at uncertain hours of the day and night. A strong party of the Jalandar mutineers (400 infantry and 200 cavalry in full equipment) invaded the Western Dun in June, but were driven out by the mere rumour that the Superintendent was leading a force against them. The peace of the district remained unbroken, save by a rare foray of the lawless herdsmen of the Trans-Siwálik jungles, five of whom were taken and hanged in one instance.*

What caused the chief inconvenience and difficulty of the Dun was the question of the supplies. A castle twelve miles broad and sixty miles long, with the rear open to the whole glacier-crowned *Oberland* of the Indo-Thibetan chain, cannot be called a small castle. None the less were the people of Mussooree in the position of a beleaguered garrison. The mountains in rear produced nothing but a little mutton, with coarse grains like millet, sufficing barely for the food of the indigenous mountaineers. The Dun had never been self-supporting; and the best lands were now being taken up for tea. Food would not be procurable for money, and money, too, was getting scarce. It has been mentioned that the Sanitaria were filled with the families of officers who were engaged in their duties down below. These gentlemen, whenever they got pay, sent it up to their families in the forms of drafts on the public treasury. The treasury was open, but was rapidly being depleted, depending as it did upon supplies forwarded from the

* *Vide* Malleson, vol. iii. pp. 419–424.

plains, which supplies had now ceased. The Superintendent was not even able to maintain communication with the Provincial Accountant-General at Agra. In this state of things, with official bankruptcy staring him in the face, the Superintendent, after consultation with his friends, adopted a plan suggested by Lieutenant Tennent, of Engineers,* and started a paper currency. It was a somewhat hopeless undertaking; but public confidence had not been entirely destroyed—so long as Spankie held his own at Sahâranpur—and the business of life had to go on somehow. The notes floated, but they floated at a discount. The ladies, and others, who presented bills at the treasury to be cashed, were naturally unwilling to be paid in a depreciated currency; the moment was critical. In this emergency the authorities of the Panjáb, ever vigilant, even where not personally responsible, came to the front, and sent several remittances of specie. But even this was not enough; and we find Mr. Spankie, amid all the cares created by the condition of his own district, pouring in supplies to the Dun, both in specie and in kind. The official narrative shows that, between the middle of May and the middle of September, he sent to the Dun no less than 3,300 maunds of grain, besides a quantity of bullocks; over 12,000 rupees to the commissariat officer; 114,000 rupees to the Superintendent of the Dun, who was thus, from this source and from the Panjáb, enabled to issue a certain proportion of specie, along with a balance in paper, until the reopening of communication with the Accountant-General.

It is time to return to Sahâranpur. On the night of the 4th June Mr. Spankie attacked the Gujars, by whom the treasury was threatened, and repulsed them with loss, burning two of their villages. On the 8th and 9th came inspiriting rumours that the Meerut garrison had at last taken the field, and then that they had beaten a body of mutineers at Gháziabad, on the Hindan, and established a junction with the main force of the British under Sir H. Barnard. Two parties were sent out to

* Since, as Colonel Tennent, the distinguished Master of the Calcutta Mint.

endeavour to cut off the mutineers of the Jalandar brigade; but, like the Superintendent of the Dun, failed to overtake their rapid flight to Dehli, which was the general rendezvous of all the mutineers. Messrs. Robertson and Plowden were next sent out against refractory villages, with such bodies of troops as could be spared; and they met with considerable success. So matters went on until the second week in July; and to a careless or over-sanguine eye it might have seemed that the trouble was over. But the end was not yet. At 8 one evening, while the Englishmen at the magistrate's house were sitting down to their well-earned meal, and deluges of monsoon-rain were falling out-of-doors, a messenger burst in with the report that MacDougall's guard had deserted their post, which was hard at hand. Major Bagot immediately hurried to the general treasury—a mile off—feeling that the desertion of the Stud-guard was ominous of a mutiny among the men of the 29th, by whom, in spite of the revolt of their main body at Morádábád, the offices there were still guarded. Followed by a number of his companions, Mr. Spankie also hastened to the spot. But the news of the advance had already reached the guard, who had decamped without plundering, and had, indeed, in their hurry, left pots and pans of their own to such an extent as fetched 300 rupees at auction next day. Seventy-nine sepoys, favoured by the weather and the darkness, escaped; a good riddance! For, though it would be utterly vain to speculate on the causes of their desertion, after so long remaining faithful, it can hardly be doubtful that their departure was felt as a sensible relief by the Europeans. The Bengal cavalry, under Wyld, had also been drawn off across the Jumna, replaced by troopers in the employ of the Patiála state. The garrison of Sahâranpur had thus been purged of all peccant humours; and a solidarity set in which was never again disturbed. On the 11th July Mr. Robertson, ever prompt to carry out the orders of his chief, went to assist the reorganisation proceeding at Rurki under Captain Read, who had taken the place of Baird Smith gone to Dehli. He there attacked and dispersed an assembly of Banjára plunderers, and thence proceeded, by Mr. Spankie's orders, to the relief of Deoband. This is an old town in the heart of the "Kháta," as the country of the worst tribes was called. The peaceable citizens had done what they could in their own defence, but had suffered severely from the audacity of the insurgents. These men were, in several instances, captured with their booty in their possession; and an examination of the town, which followed, threw some light upon the nature of the case. The quarters that had escaped plunder were those of the Gujars, the Muslims, and the labouring poor. The attack had been concentrated upon the Hindus proper, one of whose leading men was severely wounded in defending his house, while his son was carried off by the enemy before Robertson arrived. From these services the party had to be recalled. The "Nawáb" was still at his underground work, and reliable information was received by Mr. Spankie of an impending attack by the predatory classes of the vicinity reinforced by the town mob. Spankie at once took the most energetic measures. Sending for his treacherous Muslim subordinate, he thanked and promoted him, deputing him to the post of sub-collector at Nokur, in the north-western part of the district. The jail-guard, whose fidelity was doubtful, were replaced by forty Gurkhas; and the aid of a small body of British soldiers from the convalescent depôt of Landour was obtained, by whose aid tranquillity was maintained through all the excitement of the great Muhamadan celebration of the ten days of Muharam.

The "Nawáb" was completely blinded by Spankie's treatment of him. Thinking that now he had the ball at his feet, he became less guarded in his correspondence with Dehli. Spankie at last obtained satisfactory evidence of his guilt; a party of Gurkhas under Lieutenant T. Boisragon,* visiting Nokur one morning, seized this modern Agag in the midst of his office. That officer at once marched him over to Ambála, where ("according to arrangements previously made") he was brought to trial, and

* Afterwards Major-General Boisragon, and distinguished in Afghánistán.

ultimately executed by order of Mr. Barnes, the Commissioner, acting under special powers. This little incident, running like a serio-comic thread of personal interest through the official narratives, seems very characteristic of a calm, long-headed administration; and on that account, as also by reason of its own importance, it has been dwelt on at some length. The man had been a dangerous conspirator, and might have become more so had not a touch of diplomacy been mingled with the masculine resolution of the district-officer's strong character.

This was the closing scene of the local drama. But, much as Mr. Spankie had done for his own post and for the Dun, his labours were by no means confined to this immediate neighbourhood. The two elements of Muslim craft and Gujar greed extended far down into the adjoining district of Muzafarnagar.

The district of Muzafarnagar bears a general resemblance to that of Sahåranpur, from which it is only parted by an imaginary boundary on the northern side. Two canals traverse it from north to south, running parallel to the rivers Ganges and Jumna, from which they are respectively derived. On the eastern side are some Muhamadan landholders, Saiads by origin, and professing the Shiah, or Persian, form of the faith, which separates them in feeling and interest from the Indian Muslims generally. It is hard to say that the Shiahs are less fanatical, or more so, than the Sunnis; but the fact that they are a minority in India probably disposes them, however slightly, in favour of a foreign and impartial government. On the western side the estates are chiefly held by village communities. In the centre are pure Hindus and Gujars, nominally Hindus, and large clusters of Pathán clans, whose head-quarters are at Thána Bháwan, and Jalálábád.

The first disorders at the chief town were due to the weakness of the officers in charge, who, being without trustworthy followers, showed a want of initiative for which they should not be too severely blamed. A party of the 4th Irregular Cavalry, sent to their assistance, mutinied and murdered their European officer;

the bad characters rose, and committed excesses, and the British magistrates were obliged to seek refuge in the office of the sub-collector. This man, Imdád Hosen by name, belonged to the influential tribe of Saiads, named above as holding the lands on the Gangetic side of the district, and stoutly stood by the fallen authorities, for which he was afterwards handsomely rewarded.

On the 24th of June, Mr. Spankie, ever thoughtful and provident, detached one of his civil subordinates, Mr. R. M. Edwards, to take over charge of the district, and Mr. Berford, the district officer who had already before the first outbreak been an applicant for leave of absence, by reason of ill-health, at once made over his office and left. As Mr. Edwards wrote in his *Narrative*, Mr. Berford had had great difficulties to contend with, the authorities at Meerut (only thirty-three miles off) having left him not only without assistance, but even for some time without authentic intelligence.

The public business was, of course, much disorganised, nor was Mr. Edwards at first in a position to take very active steps to put matters straight. False rumours were in the air; communications were interrupted; revenue payments were backward. All this disconcerted the new district-officer, especially (as he observed) "coming as I did direct from Sahāranpur, so well and energetically kept in hand by Mr. Spankie." Mr. Edwards does not state what were the constituents and strength of his force; but he sent out parties east and west, and by their help the communications were restored, and some money collected. On the west, the chief cause of uneasiness was the town of Shámli, a place of some importance commercially and otherwise, where the leading citizens were Hindus of somewhat turbulent character; while the head of the agriculturists was a man of some influence, named Mohr Singh, who was on bad terms with the sub-collector, a gallant Pathán, by name Ibráhim Khán. Mohr Singh put himself in correspondence with the rebel court at Dehli, and thus gave rise to the confusing spectacle of a Hindu doing the work of

Muslim hostility, against a Muslim officer who was loyal to the Christian rulers.

On the 27th August, Mr. Edwards received a reinforcement from Sahāranpur. This comprised fifty bayonets of the Gurkha battalion, already mentioned as having joined Mr. Spankie there. These, from their proved loyalty and courage were most welcome, the more so as they were accompanied by two British officers. Mr. Grant had been for some time stationed at Shámli with a small party of horse, and early in September Mr. Edwards sent some infantry and two mountain-guns to his aid, following himself soon after.

In the meantime the Muhamadans of Thána Bháwan, about a day's march to the N., had broken out on hearing that one of their leaders had been executed by sentence of the court-martial at Saháranpur. Disturbance now became general in all the north and most of the west of the district; in fact, wherever the Jats were strong. On the 14th September, Mr. Edwards broke up from Shámli, leaving a few of the 1st Panjáb Cavalry to strengthen the guard of the sub-collector Ibráhim Khán, which consisted otherwise of ten troopers at home on furlough, some jail-guards and Pathán levies, in all, nearly 100 armed men. Trusting to their efforts to maintain themselves during his short absence, Mr. Edwards first moved against the fort of Burhána, which he captured. Then, reinforced by two horse-artillery guns and 100 Sikhs, he began to turn towards Shámli. But during his absence that place had been the scene of a cruel tragedy. The Thána Bháwan insurgents took advantage of the moment, and, falling on Shámli while Edwards' back was turned, surrounded the sub-collector's office. This was defended all day; but the mob was enormous, and, availing itself of the services of some gypsies who crept up under cover of screens, was able to set fire to the thatch of several buildings in the enclosure that projected over the wall. Overpowered, wearied, blinded by the conflagration, the defenders capitulated on promises that were immediately set at naught. The rebels murdered 113 persons in cold blood, and plundered the office. Mr. Edwards was prevented from immediately avenging this outrage by the most alarming reports from Muzafarnagar, on which he fell back. Neither he nor the Commissioner are good chronologers, but it would seem that about the date of the Shámli massacre Dehli was already to some extent, at least, in the possession of our troops. It is remarkable that so much audacity should have been shown at such a time, when all men who had eyes to see must have been conscious that the rebellion was about receiving its death-blow. It has been already mentioned that Mr. Edwards had been reinforced from Meerut. About the same date he also received further aid from Sahâranpur. Thus strengthened, he resolved to set out for Thána Bháwan, being under the impression that the Commissioner wished him to do so, and being advised by his military coadjutors that their force was sufficient for the purpose. He does not exactly state what that force was; but it is evident that it consisted of Sikhs, infantry and cavalry, a party of Gurkhas, and two horse-artillery guns. He was accompanied by two gallant young civil officers, Messrs. Swinton Melville and Malcolm Low, who had been sent by Mr. Spankie with the last reinforcements. Mr. Edwards neither mentions the day on which he departed, nor that on which he reached Thána Bháwan, but this latter event cannot have occurred sooner than the 16th September.* The troops, on arrival, drove in the outposts of the defenders and attempted to breach; but their guns were not of sufficient calibre, and an attempt was then made to carry the place by a rush. A storming party of Sikhs and Gurkhas was gallantly led by Captain Smith and Lieutenant Cuyler, who advanced under a smart fire of small arms from the town. Several outlying buildings were seized and occupied, and the stormers, scaling the main wall, effected their entry into the town and captured two guns. But, for some unexplained reason, the supports did not come up, and the attack had to be entirely with-

* Dehli was assaulted on the 14th. The rebels must have heard of this, as they were not fifty miles away.

drawn. The loss amounted to seventeen killed and twenty-five wounded, among whom two were British officers. In the retreat Melville and Low distinguished themselves highly by leading cavalry charges, in one of which Low was severely wounded, having been mobbed in a village lane, where he received three sabre-wounds in hand-to-hand fighting. The Commissioner afterwards attempted to throw the blame of this disaster on Mr. Spankie, who, as he originally thought, might have sent larger reinforcements to strengthen the attack. But in his printed *Narrative* (dated November 1858), he, though somewhat lamely, admitted his error, or, at least, modified his statement. The fact was, that the strength of a force for the storming of a town is a matter for the consideration of military officers alone. Major Bagot, who commanded at Sahâranpur, did not feel himself justified in detaching more of his small party, while Mr. Edwards' military advisers on the spot considered their force sufficient for the task. The fault—if fault there were—lay with the Commissioner himself, who, having first sent Mr. Edwards peremptory instructions to "proceed at once to crush the rebels," failed to countermand those instructions in time when he found, on second thoughts, that they were premature.

Further reinforcements were soon received, and the place was occupied, without resistance, before the end of September. And this was the end of the trouble in Muzafarnagar. All the loyal were amply rewarded, and such punishment was meted out to the rebels as circumstances would allow.

In addition to these exceptional doings, the district officer of Sahâranpur carried on, as best he could, the ordinary administration of his district. Money has been called "the sinews of war"; it is no less the objective of peace. During the four months that have been here hastily reviewed, all the land revenue had been collected except a balance of some fourteen per cent., which was reported on the 26th September as "in course of realisation." Criminal judicial duties were mostly performed by courts-martial, what in Europe is called "the state of siege" having been proclaimed in the district. But Mr. Spankie took care that a civil officer was always present to assist the military members of the courts. It is pleasing to be able to add that out of a population of nearly a million only ninety-five—the worst culprits, taken red-handed—were left for execution; viz. in Sahàranpur thirty-one, twenty in Rurki, forty-four in Deoband, where the violence and rapine were the worst. Most of the poor rascals were flogged and discharged.

The above facts have been derived either from the printed official *Narrative* or from personal recollections; I have also had access to private sources of unexceptionable character. Thus Colonel Baird Smith, writing three years afterwards, conveyed to Mr. Spankie the formal acknowledgments of the Christian community of Rurki, and in doing so made use of the following language:—

To Robert Spankie, Esq., C.S., late Magistrate and Collector of Saharunpore.

SIR, Calcutta, 31st July, 1860.

With reference to your demi-official of the 15th inst., I have great pleasure in expressing to you, on behalf of the European community of Roorkee, our deep sense of gratitude for the earnest and vigorous support and assistance given by you to us during the whole of the troubled period in 1857–58.

With the exception of the time I was before Delhi, I had constant opportunities of judging, from personal knowledge, of the influence of your resolute administration in maintaining peace and order within a district full of the elements of disorganisation.

Having to control the chief town of the district, with its population of about six-and-thirty thousand, many among whom were discontented and fanatical Mahommedans, with numerous other large towns restless and excited, with a rural population containing an exceptionally large proportion of turbulent aggressive and courageous tribes in active revolt against all law and order, with actual mutiny and attempted violence in the station, you had difficulties to contend with which, I have ever thought, could only have been successfully met by a rare combination of courage, decision, resource—thorough knowledge of native character, and incessant personal vigilance. Aided by your energetic subordinates, you made law respected throughout the district; saved life and property, within and beyond it, to an almost inestimable extent; for if the disaffected had mastered Saharunpore, Mussoorie must have been at their mercy with but feeble chance of resistance, and the fate of the large and chiefly helpless European community there can scarcely be matter of even momentary doubt. That you were, under God, the chief means of preventing such catastrophes has always been my conviction, and in common with many others I have felt heartily grateful to you for your efforts to avert them.

On my own behalf I may add, that among the many civil officers from whom the necessities of the case compelled me to seek assistance for the Engineer Park during the siege of Delhi, there was no one who met my requisitions, whether for men or materials, in a heartier or more earnest spirit of co-operation than yourself. The ability to complete the works necessary for the capture of Delhi within the short time actually employed, was not more a consequence of the indefatigable exertions of the troops in the trenches, than of the constant and laborious preparations systematically carried on for months beforehand. To the latter your aid was frequent and most important.

While it would be gratifying to us, who were your associates in the times of danger now gone by, to see your services recognised in any form agreeable to yourself, our estimate of those services must always remain the same; and you may be assured that the recollection of all we owed to your stout heart, and strong hand, is one of the few cheering memories of those dreary months, and will remain with most of us as long as we live.

I have the honour to be, Sir,
Your most obedient Servant,
R. Baird Smith,
late commanding at Roorkee.

It will be seen that Colonel Smith dwells upon the aid afforded to the siege-operations before Dehli. This is a feature which has been overlooked in the story as told above; but it is one that deserves attention, as showing that the safety of his own immediate neighbourhood was far from being the only subject of this officer's care.

Mr. Spankie's services were also recognised by the Home Government: the Secretary of State, Sir C. Wood, writing under date 11th June 1860, stated that he was "commanded to convey to him (Mr. Spankie) the gracious approbation of Her Majesty of his conduct during that critical period."

Recognition, it may be thought, need not have stopped here; but in times when decorations are so widely won and worn it may be a truer distinction, as Talleyrand said of Castlereagh, to be undecorated. And one may feel pretty sure that in preserving life and property, mitigating suffering, and maintaining the prestige and prerogative of his Queen and country, such a man as Robert Spankie found his truest distinction and his best reward.*

* For the sentiments of the greatest man of the class, whether as to conduct or character, see a letter by John Lawrence, under date July 21, 1858, in Bosworth Smith's *Life*, vol. ii. p. 333.

CHAPTER II.

MEERUT AND BULANDSHAHR.

THE next district, in geographical order, is that which takes its name from the town of Meerut. It is large, extending over the whole Duáb—here wider than in the more northern tracts; and it contained, at the time of the Mutiny, some two thousand square miles, supporting a population of considerably over a million.* As in Muzafarnagar, the people are divided into Jats, Gujars, Brahmans, and Muhamadans; like Saháranpur, it contains few of the *rais*, or large-landholder class. Consequently, its behaviour during the troubles of '57, has been thought to give countenance to the doctrines of the school of politicians who favour the landholder rather than the peasant. Bnt, in truth, no conclusion can be drawn from this; for some of the peasant tribes—as will presently be seen—were loyal; while in districts where land was held by powerful individuals, we shall find these also exhibiting great variety of conduct. The chief town is large, but not wealthy; the population in those days being about 75,000. At the time of the Mutiny, the garrison consisted of the 6th Dragoon Guards, 1st battalion 60th Royal Rifles, some batteries of Artillery, the 3rd Bengal Light Cavalry, the 11th and 20th Native Infantry.

Hitherto our materials have been scanty. The Superintendent of the Dun evidently thought that his task—however

* The present figures are 2,361 square miles, area; and 1,313,137, population. Both area and population have slightly varied since 1857.

favoured by fortune—did not justify any trumpet-blowing when such stirring scenes, and such noble exploits, were taking place elsewhere. In Sahâranpur and Muzafarnagar the events, though they would have been startling enough in quiet times, were chiefly confined to the efforts of a handful of Englishmen in a somewhat obscure sphere; and their chief actors were reticent men who did not care to say much about what they had done. But the work in the neighbourhood of Meerut was of a more sensational character, and filled a larger portion of space and of the public mind; and it found, consequently, more numerous and more voluminous chroniclers, so that the literature of the subject is considerable, and one has no reason to complain of the paucity of matter. *Imprimis,* there is the report of Mr. Fleetwood Williams, C.S.I., at first the Judge, but afterwards Commissioner. Then there is an interesting paper by Major Williams, of the 29th Regiment of Native Infantry, employed at the time on special civil duty, and afterwards commandant of the mounted volunteers. Lastly, there is the record of the services of that body by Mr. R. Wallace Dunlop, deservedly made C.B. for his conduct, which has been already briefly referred to.* All these narratives, however, being somewhat inaccessible, it may be acceptable if a digest of them is presented to the reader. It will form a remarkable story, illustrative both of the energy of a few Britons, and of the signal fidelity and loyalty of not a few Asiatics.

Of the conduct of those in whose hands rested the first dealing with the Meerut outbreak, as little as possible shall be said. When the men of the 3rd Cavalry had been sent to prison, for refusing to use the new cartridges, we do not find that any particular precautions were adopted. The Commissioner, Mr. Hervey Greathed, had nothing to do with details; he was merely a sort of Lord-Lieutenant, a controlling officer of the whole division—about as populous as the kingdom of Ireland †—of

* *Service and Adventure with the Khâki Risala.* Bentley, 1858.

† Area, 11,301 square miles; population, 5,141,204 (Census of 1881).

which the Meerut district was a constituent shire; and he was immediately detached to Delhi. The chief officer, or magistrate, of the district was Mr. Wallace Dunlop, who was absent on sick-leave, recruiting his health in the Himalayan *Oberland.* His *locum tenens* felt that there was danger, but was unable to do more for its prevention than placing a guard of the 20th Native Infantry over the jail where the recalcitrant troopers were confined. The Brigadier, Colonel Wilson, of the Bengal Artillery, —afterwards known as Sir Archdale Wilson, commanding the force that took Dehli,—held a responsibility divided with his immediate superior, Major General Hewett. Unfortunately, when the men of the cavalry, on the day following the imprisonment (the ever-memorable Sunday, May 10th), went down to the jail and, with the connivance of the sepoy guard, enlarged their comrades, these military commanders failed to realise either the magnitude of the peril, or the strength that lay to their hands for its encounter. In the presence of a garrison of nearly two thousand white troops, of all arms, and of many native soldiers who continued staunch and stedfast to the end, the mutineers committed excesses of blood and rapine which were only exceeded by those of the furious mob whom their example stimulated; and, during the night, the mutineers effected their escape to Dehli, to carry thither the contagion of fire and sword, while the plundering, burning, and brutality of the mob continued at Meerut till near day-break. Then, at last, a body of European troops was got together to patrol the deserted streets, to gaze at the ruined bungalows, and to collect the mutilated remains of their slaughtered countrymen and countrywomen in the theatre.

Instances of individual heroism, occurring during that night of horror, are related by the Commissioner; and it is pleasing to be able to say that they were not confined to the white people. Many natives imperilled their lives in endeavouring to save men, women, and children of the lately dominant race, and not always without success.

The remaining non-combatant Europeans now moved into a large enclosure used for a magazine and school of artillery instruction, at the eastern end of the cantonment. Into this, the contents of the treasury, which had been fortunately placed under a guard of the 60th Royal Rifles, were promptly transferred. This enclosure was speedily surrounded with an entrenchment, and became a secure refuge during the remainder of the troubles. The station, or white town, was a complete wreck, and the administration of the district lost, temporarily, to the British. But this was no more than was to be expected, Like Sahâranpur and Muzafarnagar, the Meerut district contained numerous groups of Gujar villages, whose inhabitants rose to plunder and to settle accounts with their creditors. A good many of the Jat communities to north and west imitated them; the native gentry and officials lost confidence; the reports spread were confirmed by the testimony of eye-witnesses to the ruined bungalows and deserted barracks of Meerut; authority almost vanished. Mr. Johnston, indeed, the officiating magistrate, took out a party of Carabineers (6th Dragoon Guards), on the 24th May, to punish a notorious village; the villagers fled, Johnston was killed by a fall from his horse, and (as the Commissioner records), "little was effected beyond the proof of the existence of English troops, which, more frequently [and] energetically displayed, would have checked much evil."

The place of the deceased district officer was at once assumed by a refugee from Bulandshahr, Mr. G. Dundas Turnbull, who, with energetic aid from Mr. Williams, addressed himself to remedial measures. But they met with what must have appeared an immediate discouragement. The Brigadier left, under orders from army head-quarters, on the 27th May, and he took with him a light field battery, some horse-artillery, with 200 recruits, two squadrons of the Carabineers, a wing of the Rifles, the gallant Goorkhas of the Sirmur Battalion, who had come down from Dehra, a detachment of sappers, and some native horse. Meerut was left almost without defence.

The next event was the rising of some Jats under a local leader, named Sáh Mal, who enlisted a number of escaped convicts, and other lawless persons, and began ravaging the north-west portion of the district. But soon followed what must have seemed, to the hard-pressed officials, the first bit of blue in their stormy sky. About 125 men of the 11th Native Infantry, who had remained faithful, were suspected, and ordered to depart to their homes. Nearly the whole of these poor fellows begged so hard to be allowed to remain in Government employ, that, apparently more out of compassion than of confidence, they were allowed to stay and serve as policemen in the district. Some were slain while acting in that capacity, while about ninety-nine of them remained faithful and active, "continued to do good service, collecting revenue, guarding it, escorting it into the station, fighting or threatened constantly, openly scouted and abused as often as they came into Meerut with treasure." Truly, a marvellous record; and pleasant it is to add that, on the restoration of order, these good soldiers received honours and promotion, and became the nucleus of a restored regiment of the line.

On the 11th June, Major Williams arrived at Meerut; and instead of taking refuge in the entrenchment, calmly installed himself in a house on the Mall which had escaped conflagration. Next day he was joined there by Mr. Dunlop. This intrepid officer, since he heard of the disturbances of the preceding month, had marched down from Kulu, in the mountains, proceeded *viâ* Simla and Ambála to the camp at Dehli, and thence ridden over alone—only attended by four mounted constables (natives)—through the most disturbed part of the country, and assumed charge of his district. Well might a spectator write afterwards of this:—"The facts of his return from the Hills, his trip to the rebel city, and daring ride to Meerut, showed the metal (*sic*) of the man. His energy of character," adds Major Williams, "soon turned the adverse tide of events in our favour, and shortly recovered for the Government the district that had well nigh slipped from its grasp."

The Meerut officials had, about this time, received another welcome accession, in the presence of Mr. (afterwards Sir) John Cracroft Wilson, who subsequently became a prominent colonist in New Zealand. Driven from his own district of Morádábád, which had plunged into anarchy on the mutiny of the 29th Native Infantry, this gentleman placed his whole resources at the disposal of the neighbouring district officers; and his resources were weighty. To a herculean strength, incapable of fatigue, and a heart that knew not fear, Wilson joined an influence over the natives such as those who understand them know is to be exercised by the possessor of such qualities.

Mr. Dunlop, who adds a certain graphic power of drama to his vivid description of scenes *quorum pars magna fuit*, thus notes the arrival of Mr. Wilson: "He had come to Meerut surrounded by about thirty of the 8th Irregular Cavalry, over whom he exercised an extraordinary influence. They were men of the most dangerous class . . . yet Wilson, refusing to join our Volunteers, rode about the country with these suspicious characters, making them escort treasure, or hang criminals, as might be required." After mentioning that one of the native officers of this party was afterwards found to have been, at that very time, corresponding with the Court of Dehli with a view to promoting an attack on Meerut, he thus concludes:—"W. is one of those men whose labours of a quarter of a century have been, as far as fame and fortune are concerned, nearly thrown away. His energy and ability, if engaged in any of our colonies, would have won for him a position and a name." All this was ultimately to follow. Wilson achieved both fame and fortune, and his name lives in one of the most progressive colonies of the Empire.

But it is time to speak, more particularly, of the Volunteers. Soon after Mr. Dunlop's return, he felt the necessity of supplying the defect of trained troops, and proceeded to lay before the General a project for enrolling and disciplining the Christian and other loyal inmates of the entrenchment for the purpose.

The picture that he drew was alarming. The Gujars were in open rebellion throughout the district. The Jats were generally loyal; but those of Bharaut, under Sáh Mal, had committed acts of insurrection. The whole forces thus arrayed were estimated at 15,000 fighting men. The communications with head-quarters before Dehli were seriously threatened. The revenue could not be collected; and the treasury contained only some seven thousand pounds. Meanwhile, among the Rajputs, no less than among the majority of the Jats, there still continued a feeling of attachment to the Government and the existing order of things, *quo ante*, that only needed encouragement to become actively useful. But, till this was done, the district would be almost totally disorganised: "Unless some vigorous measures are taken to assist our friends, and punish our foes, we shall be totally deserted by the mass of the people: those still faithful are becoming disgusted at our apparent apathy, and the rebellion of to-day may become a revolution.' When it is remembered that this account was given nearly six weeks after the outbreak, it will be seen that it was indeed high time for exertion.

Accordingly, a Volunteer Corps was formed, armed and equipped. It included Major Williams, commandant; Captain (afterwards Sir) Charles D'Oyly, second in command; Captain (now Major-General) E. Tyrrwhitt, adjutant; twenty-eight officers of the Civil Service and army, gentlemen privates; forty-five other British troopers; and seventeen native horsemen from cavalry regiments that had mutinied. There were also twenty-seven Christian infantrymen and sixteen faithful sepoys. They were dressed in *kháki* (dust-coloured) uniforms, and aided by a couple of mountain-train guns. Space does not admit of the introduction of Mr. Dunlop's pleasant characterisation of his comrades: the judge in his spectacles; the magistrate of Bulandshahr singing to them on their night marches, in "utter defiance of time and tune"; the High Church assistant, who "took to fighting in the grade of a trooper, as an ordinary step in nature"; the "squire," whose Meltonian equipment, and easy seat on horseback, were conspicuous in their expeditions; their manners and customs at mess, when, to put the Musalman attendants on a wrong scent, bad news was always read aloud with accompaniments of cheers and laughter. These things are side-lights, but their details would now only interest a few elderly survivors and their immediate circle of friends.

The first exploit of the Volunteers had for its object three Gujar villages notorious for their crimes. The villages were burned, and out of forty prisoners taken thirty-four were hanged after inquiry. Collections of revenue quickly signalised this first success. It was followed a few days later (8th July) by another expedition, conducted by Mr. Dunlop in person, to avenge a Gujar attack upon the Jats of Begamabad, now a station of the railway between Meerut and Dehli. Taking his troop of volunteer horsemen, fifteen sepoys, twenty native Christians armed with muskets and bayonets, and the two mountain guns, manned by native gunners, the magistrate stole upon the Gujar camp in the grey of dawn, and the Khákis fought a sharp action, storming a village that was stoutly defended, laying about them like paladins, and sparing, "carefully protecting, all women and children."

Another side of district life is presented by Mr. Dunlop, who was as humane as all brave men ought to be. In many instances, as he is obliged to confess, the Civil officer of those days had the unenviable task of singly and alone protesting against indiscriminate or injudicious punishment. "*They were the tribunes of the people*"—let that singular phrase go down as their brightest and best decoration—"and had to bear the opprobrium of supporting those whom they deemed innocent against their countrymen roused to madness." None but those who were thus engaged can tell what was the weight of this unnecessary burden, added to the unavoidable anxieties of the time. Besides having to organise and conduct all sorts of measures against the common enemy, they had the special sorrow of enduring the suspicion and hostility of their friends. Take the following illustration of this statement from Mr. Bosworth Smith's recently published *Life of Lord Lawrence.* "They were browbeaten or insulted in the cutcherry or at mess. 'What am I to do?' said J. H. Batten, the Commissioner of Cawnpore . . . to Sir James Outram who, like the best soldiers of the time, shrank from shedding blood otherwise than on the field of battle or after a legal trial. 'Do you fear God or man?' replied Sir James. 'If you fear God, do as you are doing, and bear the insults that are heaped upon you. If you fear man and the mess, let them hang their number every day.'" Dunlop was more fortunate. If he had been a man to be lightly insulted, his "mess" were not the men to do it. Yet he relates a touching story (p. 87 ff.), in which he shows that only by accident was a village in his district saved, which had not only protected Christian women, but had carried loyalty to the minutest details, such as guarding an orchard of ripe fruit because it belonged to Government.

But it is time to come to the crowning exploit of the Volunteers. The Gujars had, as we saw, received a stunning blow; remained the redoubtable Sáh Mal, the Ját "Sabahdár" of Bharaut. On the 18th July Mr. Dunlop went against him, accompanied by Melville—whom we have seen distinguishing himself in the subsequent work at Muzafarnagar—and by a force comprising two mountain guns, fifty Khákis, forty of the Rifles, and a motley band of some fifty native foot. This was but a small force to lead against Sáh Mal, who was being reinforced from Dehli (only twenty miles off) by two regiments of native infantry, 150 cavalry, and four 9-pounder guns, and who was fighting with a rope round his neck. But the magistrate trusted to two things that seldom fail against Asiatics, audacity and celerity. As he says, a severe example was needed, revenue must be collected, the Civil establishments that had been driven out must be restored. The Dehli reinforcements made one attempt to surprise Dunlop, but being foiled went back to the city. After what the Commissioner justly characterises as a display of "rather rash zeal," in which he confessedly got the worst of it, Mr. Dunlop had the satisfaction of joining his main body near Bharaut, where they were presently attacked by the whole country-side. The Khákis immediately charged, and killed thirty of the enemy, who retired, followed by the whole force, the Rifles skirmishing and driving the foe out of the trees and sugar-cane which masked the village. Sáh Mal now hastened to the encounter with his main strength: but he was singled out and slain by a young planter named Tonnochy; and then the little body (" grand " total 149) advanced on the village, driving the enemy before them. Mr. Dunlop and his followers remained masters of the field, having scattered a hostile array of 3,500 men, of whom 450 in all were slain. "Sáh Mal's head being stuck upon a pole inspired our native friends with mingled satisfaction and dread." Supplies came freely in, and revenue was once more collected. Sardhana was next visited; Narpat Singh, another rebel leader, was attacked, and killed fighting; and a strong detachment of loyal sepoys was left for the protection of the Palace.* Meantime, Cracroft Wilson continued his independent labours on the eastern side of the district, on one occasion carrying off Rs. 14,000 in the teeth of a large body of insurgents.

On the 28th August an attack was made on Galaoti, in which the Carabineers bore a distinguished part: but this belongs more properly to the Bulandshahr narrative. Fired by these examples, the Commissioner next attempted an expedition against Murádnagar, on a plan of his own; it was only partially successful, and a very pessimist account will be found in Dunlop's book (p. 136). The date of this affair was 17th September. Dehli was now being assaulted; and to the anxiety on this account was added that caused by the critical state of affairs in Muzafarnagar. But both were soon removed.

* Built by the celebrated Begam Samru, and now the property of Lord and Lady Forester.

The Khákis heard of the fall of Dehli as they were on their way to take part in the final occupation of Thána Bháwan (v. *sup.*), and on their return to Meerut they were honourably disbanded, after a short but glorious service, in the course of which they had completely reorganised their own district, and aided their neighbours, south and north.

About the same time occurred the last fighting on a large scale among the people of the district. The Jats of Bhatauna, on the southward side, were attacked by a strong force of rebels and mutineers from Málagarh (a rebel centre in the Bulandshahr district). But the village appears to have been walled, for the Jats beat off their assailants after a gallant struggle in which the defenders lost twenty-five killed and wounded. Málagarh—of which we shall hear more anon—was evacuated on or about the 28th September; and soon traffic recommenced, the mails began to run, and no sign but ruins and tombs remained at Meerut to show where, " with numbers decreasing as the danger increased, a little band of Europeans, amidst thousands of rebels and within reach of Dehli, maintained the name of their country and the authority of Government." (Commissioner's *Narrative*, para. 331.)

The district of Bulandshahr is the next section of the Duáb, and is nearly the same size as that of Meerut. But, while the numerical strength of the population is not much inferior, it is differently constituted. The western part of the district, in the Jumna, is full of Gujars, of a particularly untamed and troublesome kind: but the Jats are much less frequent than in districts further north; and many of the estates, instead of being the constituents of groups of villages held by connected communities, are in the hands of comparatively wealthy landholders, some of whom are the descendants of Hindus converted to Islam. The tract to the northward, known familiarly as the *Bari Basti*, was the home of a hardy tribes of Mohamadans, from whom many recruits used to be obtained for the irregular cavalry. To the west and north-west, many villages were held by a Christian landlord, a son of Colonel James Skinner, C.B., the famous leader of partisan horse in Lake's time.

The district had just been made over by Mr. G. D. Turnbull, mentioned above, to Mr. Brand Sapte. Mr. Turnbull had not left. The other civilian officers were Messrs. Alfred Lyall (since the distinguished Lieutenant-Governor of the Provinces, and K.C.B.) and Swinton Melville, whose gallant conduct in two other districts has already been briefly noticed. Mr. Sapte had a detachment of the 9th Native Infantry from Aligarh, under Lieutenant Ross, and endeavoured further to strengthen his force by raising local cavalry. But all in vain. On the 21st May, Mr. Sapte, having heard of the mutiny of the head-quarters of the 9th at Aligarh, made an attempt to carry off the cash from his treasury to Meerut, but he was attacked by a multitude of Gujars, and forced to fly, accompanied by Mr. Melville and a few native troopers, without being able to know what had become of his remaining comrades. He reached Meerut the following morning, where he had the satisfaction of being joined during the day by Messrs. Ross, Turnbull, and Lyall.

As soon as he was gone, the Gujars burnt down his house and the rest of the European "station," let loose the inmates of the jail, and, with their assistance, destroyed the public offices and records therein. But, on the 25th, Mr. Sapte returned with some horsemen, and found the Sirmur Battalion (now the 1st Gurkhas), who had halted at Bulandshahr on their way to Dehli. Besides Ross and Lyall, he was accompanied on his return by Captain Tyrrhwitt, of the 14th Irregular Cavalry: the same who afterwards acted as adjutant of Dunlop's Volunteers. They lost no time in inflicting punishment on some of the plunderers whom they identified; and reconnoitred the position of Mr. Skinner at Biláspur, who fortunately proved to be safe and sound in a well-fortified enclosure. On the 27th their cavalry, for the most part, deserted; and next day Major Reid (now Sir C. Reid, K.C.B.) was obliged to leave with his trusty Gurkhas. The important town of Sikandrabad, eight miles west of Bulandshahr, was immediately sacked by the Gujars; and the landlord of Málagarh, a strong place four miles to the north, began to block the Meerut road. This man (who was nearly connected with the King of Dehli), though he did not at first openly break with the British, did not attempt to conceal that he had received orders from the rebel court to take charge of the district; and his attitude soon became so openly hostile that Sapte, whose force was by this time reduced to twenty men, deemed it advisable to move once more in the direction of Meerut. The European officers reached Galaoti, about twelve miles west of Bulandshahr, on the 10th June, but next morning received news which led them to return once more. On reaching Bulandshahr they found their entry disputed, and a number of men with muskets, and three pieces of cannon, drawn up across the mouth of the main street. These they boldly faced, charging up to within thirty yards of the guns, in doing which they had several horses killed by grape. Finding themselves abandoned by their escort, they then slowly retreated upon Galaoti, having on the way dispersed a force from Málagarh which attempted to cut them off.

Thus, then, there were at last two kings of Brentford; and the British ruler was, for the time, deposed in favour of the Málagarh man, Wali Dád Khán—"Willie Dods," as he became known to the European soldiers employed in those parts—whose fort was subsequently to acquire an evil notoriety. "Málagarh," so writes Mr. Sapte, "became the resort of all the disaffected, far and near. Khurja and Aligarh were occupied by the followers of the rebel Nawáb, to whose standard many of the fanatic Musalmáns of the Bari Basti hastened to flock. The fort is about nine hundred yards from the road, which was consequently commanded by the guns, of which Wali Dád possessed six at the commencement of the outbreak. Communication with Agra" (then the head-quarters of Government) "was effected with extreme difficulty; for so well was the whole line of the road and its vicinity watched, that scarcely a man could pass without being intercepted. . . . This rebel really became a formidable foe."

Mr. Sapte and his companions had fallen back on Meerut, where they remained, serving as troopers in the Volunteer Horse, until the end of August. On the 28th of that month they returned to Galaoti, with the expedition already referred to in the description of events at Meerut. It had been ascertained that Wali Dád had posted 400 horse, with 600 of his infantry, and about 1,000 insurgent Gujars, about nine miles from Hápur on the Agra road, and their pickets had been advanced to Galaoti. A force of the strength noted below* was sent to clear the road, and they advanced on the morning of the 29th, masked by some loyal Jats from Bhatauna. The enemy's pickets were driven in by the Carabineers, who sabred forty of them; the riflemen then advanced through the standing crops on each side of the road, which they cleared of rebels as they went: the guns and cavalry kept pace along the road. Thus they fought their way to near Málagarh, and drove away the enemy with a loss of seventy-two killed, besides many wounded, without a life being lost on the British side, and only five men wounded. The force returned to Meerut next day.

On the 28th September, Mr. Sapte heard of the evacuation of the fort of Málagarh, and immediately returned to Bulandshahr, in company with Brigadier Greathed's column from Dehli. On the way an engagement took place with the mutineers from Jhánsi, in which Mr. Lyall so distinguished himself in a cavalry charge as to obtain honourable mention in despatches. Málagarh was occupied, and on the 1st October was demolished—a useful act, that was clouded by a melancholy incident, The explosion was conducted by Lieutenant Home, of Engineers, one of the few survivors of the gallant exploit at the Cashmere Gate at Dehli. This heroic young officer—who on that memorable occasion had entitled himself to the Victoria Cross—lost his life by

* 2 H. A. guns; 2 M. T. guns; 50 Carabineers; 30 Khákis; 50 H. M. 60th; 20 armed Bandsmen; 15 Sikh sepoys.

the premature ignition of the exploding train in this "petty fortress."

The restoration of order was not immediate. Mr. Sapte's first act, after his final reinstatement was of a romantic, though somewhat profitless order. Tidings having been received that a Christian girl was concealed at a village not far off, in the house of a mutinous trooper, the magistrate proceeded to the spot with a party of horse. The villagers came out to oppose him; many of them being mutineers still wearing their old uniforms. A combat ensued, in which some were killed and others taken prisoners, and afterwards—rather unnecessarily, as it may now be thought—executed by sentence of court-martial. After a tedious search, the fair fugitive was discovered; but she asserted that she had married her captor, the trooper Khuda Baksh, and, on her own earnest prayer, was allowed to remain. "I did not force her away," observes Mr. Sapte, with some *naïveté,* "but left her with the assurance that her husband would be hanged whenever he was caught." There is nothing said as to the fulfilment of this grim valediction: let us hope that Khuda Baksh was never caught, and that the fond pair lived happily ever afterwards.

Next day Mr. Sapte returned to Bulandshahr; where, being ably supported by Lieutenant-Colonel Farquhar, with the right wing of the First Beloch Battalion, and by a body of Pathan horse under Major Stokes, he continued to do good and useful service. Across the Ganges, now daily dwindling and becoming fordable in many places, lay the districts of Rohilkhand, still in the hands of rebels grown somewhat desperate for want of that amnesty which John Lawrence vainly sought to extract from the bewildered Government of Calcutta. All through that winter, and up to April, when Mr. Sapte was transferred to Meerut, the rebels marched distracted, trying to pass the river and obstruct the reorganisation of the Duáb. But Mr. Sapte had now the upper-hand, and he maintained it. One of the Musalmán landholders, the Nawáb of Chitári, gave active assistance, as did some of the villagers; and Mr. Sapte not only guarded the fords, but collected the revenue, and restored order throughout his district. In all these efforts he was ably seconded by Mr. Lyall, of whom he ultinately reported that, though but a young officer, he had "evinced a sound judgment and discretion not always met with even in men of far greater experience." To this praise, readers of the narrative will add a special admiration for valour and resolution; and it is gratifying to Sir A. Lyall's friends of those days to think that he has gone on, *qualis ab incepto*, distinguished by a rare combination of qualities, until he has attained to the highest elevation that the Service affords.

Mr. Sapte also obtained well-deserved reputation and honour. In addition to being transferred to the agreeable and much-coveted post of District Officer of Meerut, when Mr. Dunlop went on furlough, he became in due time a Companion of the Bath. These honours, which were not always bestowed with equal discrimination, were well-deserved in the case of Mr. Sapte, of whom his official superior, Mr. Fleetwood Williams, very propeily made honourable mention in his *Divisional Narrative*. His remarkable tenacity in confronting the Málagarh rebel and returning time after time to his perilous guard, after being driven out by overwhelming force, received just commendation. And so did the *sangfroid* with which he and his gallant comrades made head against the enemy, whenever they had the faintest chance, "not hesitating to charge guns pouring grape upon them in a narrow road."

It was this cheery manhood, this sanguine, hopeful "pluck," combining with an unfailing sense of duty, that, amid constant defeat and disappointment, made the peculiarity of the finally-triumphant defence of Bulandshahr.

CHAPTER III.

AGRA, ALIGARH, AND MUTTRA.

The next district, according to the map, is that of Aligarh, but the events there were not sufficiently grave to furnish much matter for a special narrative. The same may be said of the adjoining district of Muttra—or, Mathura, as now written—and the magistrates of these two districts, Messrs. Bramly and Thornhill, have described their mutiny administration with such brevity and lack of literary skill, as to render the events there less interesting, even, than might otherwise be the case. Good men were there who did good deeds; but they are in the same condition as the brave who lived their lives before Agamemnon. It will therefore be enough if we briefly consider Aligarh and Muttra in connection with Agra, to which they served as satellites.

The district of Aligarh is named after an old fort about two miles north of the city of Koil. Originally built under the Mughal Government, this fort had been strengthened by the Mahrattas and their French officers; but it was taken by Lake in 1803 by a brilliant *coup-de-main*, as described, under the chapter of Láswari, in Colonel Malleson's *Decisive Battles of India*. It was not occupied during the early part of the Rebellion, and need not further detain us here. About half-way between the town and the fort stands the "Station," a small collection of bungalows grouped about the public offices.

At the time of the outbreak, several neighbouring estates

were in the hands of British planters, amongst whom the most noticeable were Messrs. Paterson Saunders and John O'Brien Tandy,* cousins, and men of great spirit and influence.

The force present in May consisted of 300 men of the 9th Native Infantry, commanded by Major Eld; reinforced on the news of the Meerut outbreak by the right wing of the 1st Regiment of Cavalry of the Gwalior Contingent, under Captain Alexander. On the evening of the 20th the Infantry broke into mutiny, burned the offices, and carried off about thirty thousand pounds in specie, with which they marched off to the insurgent head-quarters in Dehli. The officers, civil and military, were allowed to depart to Háthras, a town south of Aligarh, on the road to Agra, which they reached in safety. Here they were joined by a planter named Nichterlein, and other refugees, Mr. Nichterlein's son having been killed on the way. On the 26th they were reinforced by a body of mounted Volunteers raised by Mr. Saunders, and commanded by Mr. Wilberforce Greathed,† of the Bengal Engineers, one of three brothers who took very distinguished parts in the events that were going on in the neighbourhood. Other members of this little force were Messrs. Arthur Cocks,‡ C.S., J. O'B. Tandy, Harington, and Castle; Ensign Ollivant (since a prominent officer of the Provincial Police), and Ensign Marsh. These gallant fellows, having performed the main object of their expedition—which was the relief of a factory—proceeded to Abigarh, where they reinstated Mr. William Watson, the then magistrate (who afterwards died of cholera in Agra Fort), and remained there till the 2nd of July, when they were driven out by overwhelming invasions, and retired to Agra.

Meanwhile, Mr. Mark Bensley Thornhill, of Muttra, who had taken the field with a body of Bhurtpore troops under Captain

* I believe Mr. Tandy was not actively concerned in the management of these estates, but had come up from Calcutta on a visit.

† Afterwards Colonel Greathed, C.B., Secretary to Government, North-West Provinces.

‡ Already distinguished during the Panjab campaign of 1848–9.

Nixon, was recalled to his chief station by news that the detachment of the 44th Native Infantry had mutinied, murdered Lieutenant Burlton, their commandant, and plundered the Treasury. This occurred on the 26th. On the morning of the 30th Mr. Thornhill returned; but finding the Station ruined and deserted, proceeded to Agra to seek assistance. Not succeeding, he returned next day—having been repeatedly shot at on the road—buried Burlton's body (which he found naked in a ditch near the ruins of the Treasury), and endeavoured, with the aid of some wealthy native bankers, to restore order. In this he was only moderately successful. Fifty thousand pounds had been carried off; the jail-birds had broken loose; the police had mutinied, and spread abroad with arms in their hands; many of the zemindars refused to pay revenue, and set themselves up in all directions as Rájas. Thornhill seems to have done what he could in these trying circumstances. He took up his quarters in the city, which he protected by barricades; he raised fresh police, and, on being joined by some of the Contingent of the Kota State under Captain Dennys, proceeded into the district, and seized one of the ringleaders of the rural revolt, who was immediately hanged for the discouragement of the others. Seven more were executed soon after, and a number of minor offenders severely flogged. The magistrate further evinced his resources by submitting to the Lieutenant-Governor at Agra a plan for utilising the loyal landowners, by giving them special powers to enforce authority, which was sanctioned and carried out. These measures, working surely, if slowly, gradually brought about some semblance of tranquillity.

To return to Aligarh. It has been said that the Volunteers remained there till the 2nd of July. That is, however, not strictly true, though so stated by Mr. Bramly. The fact is, that only eleven so remained, the majority having been recalled to Agra on the 21st of June. On the 30th of that month, these eleven gentlemen performed a notable exploit. Receiving intimation that the rabble of Koïl were on the way to attack them in a factory where they were temporarily quartered, flying the green flag of Islám, and sworn to have their heads posted over the city-gates by nightfall, they mounted their horses to receive the visit. Presently the advanced guard, a body of more than 500 men, were perceived marching up the road. Watson's party immediately charged. Fourteen of the assailants were slain; the rest fled in every direction, and their stragglers fell into the hands of the villagers by the wayside, who stripped them to the skin. The names of Watson's intrepid comrades are given in the note,* for such a deed ought to be fully recorded. Outram was son of the famous Sir James, whom he succeeded in the baronetcy.

Marsh and Tandy were doomed men. The former, a most promising young officer, was shot in a subsequent skirmish. On the same occasion, Tandy, reckless, as Irishmen of good birth are apt to be at the sight of combat, jumped his horse over the wall of an orchard crowded with fanatics, by whom he was immediately cut to pieces. Saunders—an equally fearless man—lived for many years after; and most, if not all, of the others still (1883) survive to look back, as on a dream, to those stirring times.

It is unnecessary to dwell for the present on events in these outlying districts. Early in July Watson and Thornhill were both driven from their districts and forced to take refuge in the fort of Agra, to which place our scene now changes.

Agra, at the time of the outbreak, was the official capital of the province of Hindustan proper, or "North-West Provinces," to use the technical term. Here were stationed the Lieutenant-Governor, at that time the Hon. John Russell Colvin, a man of signal ability; the Chief, or "Sudder," Court of Judicature; the Board of Revenue; and the head-quarters of the several departments of the public service. The garrison comprised a battery of Horse Artillery, a newly-raised battalion

* A. Cocks, C.S., Outram, C.S., Ensign Ollivant, Ensign Marsh, Messrs. P. Saunders, J. O'B. Tandy, H. B. Harington, Hind, Castle, and Burkinyoung, Stewart Clark, M.D

of Foot—the Company's 3rd European Regiment—and the 44th and 67th Native Infantry. This force was commanded by Brigadier Polwhele, and the chief civil officer of the district was the Hon. Robert Drummond (brother of Viscount Strathallan). The population consisted of about 150,000 souls, of which over 2,000 were Christians.

On learning the news of the mutiny at Muttra, Mr. Drummond, a man of strong character, at once promised the sanction of the Government to the disarming of the sepoy regiments. This was effected on the morning of the 31st May without bloodshed, and the men dispersed "on leave of absence." This step was followed by the enrolment of the Christians capable of bearing arms; expeditions were sent in the direction of the Bhurtpore frontier, and order was maintained, *tant bien que mal*, for about a fortnight. On the 15th June the force stationed at Sindhia's capital, under the designation of "the Gwalior Contingent," mutinied, and the example was followed by the detachment of that force which had been hitherto serving in the Agra district. Soon after came news of the mutinies at Nasirabad and Nimach, and of the approach of a strong body of the mutineers from those places. According to the invariable practice, these men were to join the great gathering at Dehli; but, encouraged by sympathisers at Agra, they had resolved to make a slight deviation in order to capture and kill the English at Agra on their way. This would be a good feather to wear in their caps as they presented themselves before the King, besides gratifying the instincts for slaughter and loot, which were just then very active in sepoy bosoms. Their hopes, however, were destined to be disappointed.

The encounter between the mutineers and the defenders of Agra has been described in the histories of the period (notably in Malleson's *Indian Mutiny*), and has no special claim to be noticed here, but for two reasons. One is that, though successful in so far that the mutineers were repulsed from Agra, it was attended by disasters; the other that, while not remarkable as a specimen of military skill, it was signalised by much dash and heroism on the part of men usually falling under the tite of "non-combatants."

The enemy were met at Sucheta, being computed at 2,000 foot, 600 horse, and ten field-pieces. To these the Agra garrison could only oppose 600 bayonets, thirty-three mounted volunteers, and six Horse Artillery guns. Still, Englishmen in India had often been victorious over far greater odds than that; and the Brigadier was quite justified in assuming the offensive. Of the action that ensued it need only be here observed that every conceivable advantage was thrown away. With the exception of a charge by Major Prendergast, who lost twelve out of his eighteen civilian troopers, the British were demoralised by being kept back till their guns became useless by the explosion of their tumbrils and the death of their officer, the gallant Captain D'Oyley; and the troops had to be eventually retired from the field, and escorted into their quarters in the fort by the volunteer infantry left behind as a reserve. Two officers and thirty-nine men were killed, and ninety-nine of all ranks wounded. But the enemy had also suffered, and they turned from their vainglorious purpose and went their way to Dehli, *re infectâ*.

It is no doubt to be regretted that a bolder front was not at once assumed. But the Council was distracted. Over 5,000 persons were now crowded into the narrow limits of the fort, which became a scene of the utmost confusion. "Loose horses were fighting and galloping about; artillery-cattle lying wounded and dying with thirst; drunken soldiers bivouacking in the rain." From the ramparts a circle of fire was seen, denoting the destruction of the European habitations. It was not till the third day that, on urgent invitation from well-wishers in the city, the local authorities were permitted to emerge from this dismal shelter. An armed demonstration was carried through the city on the 8th July, and "from this moment," says the author of the District Narrative, "rapine, murder, and outrage ceased." It was not too soon. During the three days and nights of inactivity no less than seventeen men, women, and children of European blood had been gratuitously and brutally murdered by the police and other rascaldom of the native quarters.

The writer hopes that he will not be charged with *esprit de corps* of an unjust sort if he invites the observation that these calamities were in no degree due to the civil officers. Drummond, though his policy in some respects incurred grave disapproval, had energy enough and to spare. March-Phillipps and Oldfield* charged like Paladins with Prendergast—the only thing bold that was done in the battle of Sucheta. Mr. E. A. Reade, senior member of the Revenue Board, was conspicuous wherever calm courage and sagacity could be of use.

On the 10th July Mr. Drummond was removed with promotion (at that time nominal) to the post of Civil and Sessions Judge at Banda, a district then in full revolt. Mr. March-Phillipps succeeded him in charge of the Agra district. A council of the leading native citizens was convened by Mr. Reade, and the place of the regular police—who had utterly betrayed their trust—was taken by the heads of the various *Mohalas,* or wards, of the city, under the control of a trustworthy *Kotwál* named Rája Rám. It is very noteworthy that this officer, who was appointed on the recommendation of the headmen of the native community, proved in every way faithful and efficient: for we have here a specimen of the elective system tried probably for the first time in an Indian city, and certainly under the most searching conditions.

But, if the state of Agra itself had become reassuring, far otherwise were the feelings caused by a survey of the district at large. The inaction that followed immediately on the battle of Sucheta had given the signal for universal anarchy, of which the first symptom was an almost simultaneous attack upon all

* Shot through the lungs, this officer recovered, and is now (1883) the Hon. Mr. Justice Oldfield, Puisne Judge of the High Court, N.W.P.

the outposts where authority was represented in the district. Some of the native officials joined the mutineers, others retired to their homes in distant places; those who remained and tried to do their duty were hard pressed and, generally speaking, driven away. In one case—the sub-collector having fled—the very landholder whom he professed to fear took charge of the office, and protected the records, and the town itself, until the troubles came to an end. So various are the workings of human nature!

The first efforts of the British authorities were directed to Fatihpur-Sikri, the old country palace of the Mughal emperors, about twenty miles west of Agra, where a strong party of rebels had established themselves. The old town is steep and narrow, while the palace buildings are massively built of stone, on the top of a rock a mile and a half long, standing in a walled park. Decently defended, they might have afforded a stubborn resistance; and it was but a slender column that Agra could spare for their reduction. A body of fifty British bayonets and thirty mounted volunteers, under the command of Captain Patton, accompanied Mr. Phillipps to Fatihpur on the 29th of July. They were attacked in the narrow streets of the town by a strong force of Mewátis, a tribe of predatory Muslims, who at first drove them out. Being reinforced in the open, the magistrate and his men charged, killing fourteen of the enemy, and capturing two prisoners, who were afterwards tried and executed. The Mewátis evacuated the palace, in which Government offices were at once established. On the 10th August, a similar expedition was sent to Itmádpur, under the joint magistrate, Mr. W. H. Lowe, and order was restored there. Shortly after, the eastern border towards Mainpuri—a revolted district—was settled; and here, also, the offices were re-opened; while, on the north, matters were restored about the same time by the influence of a loyal native nobleman, the Raja of Awa-Misa. Greater difficulty was experienced in the parts to the south-east, which were too remote to be dealt with by the dwindling garrison of Agra Fort; but here again aid was obtained from the Bhadaurias, a powerful clan of Rajputs, whose chief, though not himself a man of much force of character, was kept straight by a well-disposed councillor. So wore on the month of August, during which the Christian inhabitants of Agra, many of them women and children, accustomed to every comfort when they were not sent to the hills for the summer, were exposed to the ills of climate in the most extreme form. In close rooms, or in tents under broiling heat and pelting rain, the ladies bravely bore their parts, tending the sick and wounded, and winning the respect of all.

After the middle of September, disturbances were resumed by fugitives from Dehli. Some made their way across the Jumna to Rohilkand; others, under Prince Firoz,* assembled at Dhaulpur, about half-way between Gwalior and Agra; and finally, about the beginning of October, advanced to attack the fort. Before they could carry out their purpose, however, Colonel E. Greathed, of the 8th Foot, had arrived at Háthras with a British column of all arms. Towards this officer the eyes of the British at Agra were now anxiously turned; and on the 9th October the best information available was sent to him, in pursuance of which he hastened on. He arrived in the nick of time. On the morning of the 10th, Greathed crossed the bridge of boats, and proceeded with his column to the brigade parade-ground, south of the fort, at the very instant that the Prince's columns, in entire ignorance of his arrival, were approaching from Dhaulpur. The collision was short, sharp, and decisive. "Such was the promptitude with which the different arms formed into position, that the artillery of the right flank replied to the fourth gun of the enemy." The battery was charged, and taken, by twenty-five of the 9th Lancers, under Captain Green, who unhappily was killed in the *mêlée*; the rebels soon took to flight, and were pursued for eight miles. They lost 1,000 men, in killed alone; the British

* Afterwards transiently troublesome in Etáwa and elsewhere; ultimately believed to have retired to Mecca.

loss amounting to eleven killed and fifty-four wounded, four of whom were officers. This is a military incident which will be found fully described in the standard histories; it has been only referred to here because a certain amount of blame has been sometimes thrown upon the civil officers, on account of their not furnishing Greathed with closer details of the enemy's movements. The evidence recorded in Mr. Phillipps' narrative shows that they gave all information that it was in their power to obtain, and that the surprise was perfectly unavoidable.

It remains to add that Rája Rám, the new Kotwál, kept the city quiet during these events, and made public proclamation of the result of the battle as soon as he became aware of it. From that moment no further disturbance took place in the city, and the reorganisation of the district began to assume the character of "a question of time."

The remaining events in Agra, and the adjacent districts of Aligarh and Muttra, may be briefly disposed of. Mention has been made of the defensible position of the old palace of Fatihpur-Sikri, so familiar to sight-seers. A body of mutineers from Dehli was harboured there by the Mewátis, already mentioned as giving trouble in the same locality; and an expedition went to dislodge them towards the end of October. Colonel Cotton commanded, and carried the place by storm, after a severe resistance in which the defenders lost eighty of their number. The column then moved on in the direction of Muttra, putting down recalcitrant landholders, and restoring the local officers and establishments. On the 27th of November, Mr. Phillipps took out a small force into the ravines of the Jumna on the opposite (eastern) direction, where forty-five policemen had been massacred in one night while engaged in an inquiry. Mr. Phillipps was only partially successful in this demonstration, as his force was recalled to the city before its full purpose had been attained. The city had been, by this time, surrounded by a wall; but no precautions appear to have given complete satisfaction. The ultimate result of the revolt, for Agra, was that the seat of government was removed to the less central, but more strategic, region of Allahabad, where it has continued ever since.

In the meanwhile, the districts of Aligarh and Muttra were gradually cooling down. After the battle of Sucheta had somewhat ceased to depress the military spirit at Agra, a small force under Major Montgomery was sent out, to which Mr. Cocks, C.S., was attached as Special Commissioner. The very presence of this little force produced a healthy effect on public opinion, "showing them," as Mr. Bramly naively puts it, "how vastly inferior they were to the men they were attempting to crush." On the 10th August, Montgomery marched towards Hathras, which was threatened by Ghaus Mohamad, a deputy of Walidad the "Subah" of Málagarh. The traders of Hathras, inspired by the example of a blind pensioner, named Chaubé Gansiam Das (who was afterwards killed), exhibited a bold front; and Mr. Cocks, having occupied the place, assumed the offensive, and marched out to attack the enemy, assembled near the town of Koil. A fight ensued, in which the enemy were defeated and put to flight, with the loss of their "Maulvi," or spiritual guide. But the fall of Dehli in September brought back the elements of disorder, for a time at least; and Major Montgomery had to fall back on Agra before the tide of maddened mutineers pouring out from the rebel stronghold. After the defeat of Prince Firoz by Greathed, on the 10th October, Mr. Cocks returned to Aligarh, bringing with him Mr. Bramly, who had succeeded the gallant Watson in the office of district magistrate.* These officers were accompanied by a force of 150 British bayonets and 100 stout Sikhs. The old fort of Aligarh was cleared out, and utilised as a barrack; the city was held by a Jat chief, with

* It is curious that Watson, Saunders, and Tandy had all rebel blood in their own veins: the first from Colclough of Wexford, the second and third from Napper Tandy

a strong force of constables; and the collection of the revenue began to proceed in the usual course.

The condition of the Muttra district was for awhile less satisfactory. The country-side was overrun by mutineers; and although Mr. Thornhill's plan of administering through the local chiefs was partially successful, there were many parts which continued more or less lawless throughout the entire period of his absence at Agra. On the 5th October, however, he returned to the district, making his temporary head-quarters at Saidábád, and there taking prisoner a ringleader, who was promptly hanged. On the 1st November he got back to Muttra, under convoy of Colonel Cotton's column above mentioned, and availed himself of its aid to punish some refractory villages. The restoration of order speedily ensued.

At the same time, Mr. Phillipps was doing what he could in the Agra district, while Mr. Bramly was similarly employed in that of Aligarh. Large bodies of mutinous troops continued to cross into Rohilkand, or march distractedly back. These were occasionally caught and chastised by flying columns—a state of things which was somewhat exciting, and delayed the calming of the public mind necessary for the complete resumption of peaceful life. At length, in March 1858, a strong column marched down under Major-General Penny, commanding the division *; and no further incidents are recorded in regard to this portion of the Duáb.

Of the behaviour of the native population during this period, Mr. Bramly observes that it was generally "apathetic." A number of ex-landholders resumed estates from which they had been dispossessed in course of law; "that the people plundered when they suddenly found authority overthrown by the mutinous troops, and anarchy ready-made, was natural." But on the whole, here, as in most other places, the attitude was that of expectation, and order was restored as soon as the elements

* This officer was soon after killed by an ambuscade in the Etah district, his death being instantly avenged.

of disorder disappeared. Nevertheless, it is easy to see that the civilians in all three districts had arduous tasks set before them. It is hard to say which were the most tried: the officers of Muttra and Aligarh, left to their own resources among hordes of semi-barbarians tempted in every evil way; or those of Agra, controlled by superior authority, and hampered, to a considerable extent, by military inefficiency.

CHAPTER IV.

MAINPURI AND ETÁWA.

North-east of Agra lies the district of Mynpoory—or Mainpuri, as now spelt—which affords but scanty material for our narrative, but that little of a somewhat peculiar character. The district officer was Mr. John Power, a name full of pleasant recollections to all who remember the stately presence, the dignified demeanour of one who, though he has been called "the Indian Brummell," was a man of a far higher type than his English predecessor. A dandy Mr. Power certainly was, but it was not in a cockney way by any means, his elegance being of a massive and monumental character. The special commissioner, Mr. Cocks, who was at that time district judge, represents Mr. Power, on the 19th May as "rushing into the room where he [Mr. Cocks] was sleeping, to inform him that he had just heard of the mutiny of the 9th Native Infantry at Aligarh." That might be Mr. Cocks' recollection of the event eighteen months after (his report bears date 18th November 1858), but Mr. Power recorded at the time (*v.* his letter in the supplement dated Mynpoory, the 25th May 1857, in the first excitement) that it was on the 22nd that the news reached him, and that he "immediately *proceeded* to Mr. Cocks' house to consult him." Mr. Cocks was certainly wrong in the date; Mr. Power could not be mistaken, writing at the time; and the word "proceed" is so much more in accordance with Mr. Power's usual bearing, that we may be sure that the "rush" is a mistake also. Mr. Power could not, under any circumstances, have "rushed" in any direction; indeed, had the news by any chance reached him in his dressing-room, he would not have even "proceeded" to announce it to anyone until his toilet was completed to the last button, and the last touch of the hair-brush.

The result of the consultation was that "fourteen females, consisting of ladies, sergeants' and writers' wives, with their children (an unlimited number), left" for Agra, which they reached in safety. The military force—consisting of three companies of the mutinous 9th—was then taken out under Lieutenant de Kantzow, a very gallant young officer, a small guard being left at the Treasury. It was now past four in the morning of the 23rd, and Lieutenant Crawford, the senior officer, followed the route taken by de Kantzow, with the intention of joining the force, which was to encamp at Bhaongaon, about eight miles off. Scarcely had the civilians (Messrs. Cocks and Power, and James Power,* Dr. Watson and the chaplain, the Rev. P. Kellner), lain down to get a little sleep, when Crawford galloped back with the information that his men were in open mutiny, had fired their muskets at him, and had probably murdered de Kantzow.

Through the pretty little "station" of Mainpuri flows the Isan, a small stream, which the road leading from the officers' bungalows to the public offices crosses by a masonry bridge. Here Mr. Power took post, accompanied by his brother, and here they were joined by Dr. Watson and two or three European subordinates. Meantime, de Kantzow had not been murdered, though his men mutinied and defied his orders; many muskets were levelled at him, but the aim was always diverted by the better-disposed sepoys, de Kantzow being of a frank and generous character with many friends among the men. Dragging him with them, the mutineers returned to their lines, loading the spare ammunition contained there on camels which they appropriated for the purpose. De Kantzow's nerve never failed him; urgently he appealed to the men to return to

* A younger brother of Mr. Power's at that time serving as his assistant.

their duty, and restrain the excesses of the lawless. Heedless of his appeals, they marched to the treasury, still taking him along with them. Here they were met by the jail-guard and native officials, who prepared to resist them, and gave de Kantzow all the assistance that could be expected from under thirty untrained men acting against ten times their number of infuriated soldiers. "For three dreary hours he stood against the rebels at the imminent peril of his life." Meanwhile, the English at the bridge, half-a-dozen in number, had been joined by Rao Bhawáni Singh, cousin of the rájá—the local head of the Chanhán Rajputs—with a small escort. This small force, the Rao was persuaded, would be insufficient to reinforce de Kantzow; and a message presently came from the heroic young man begging them not to run the hazard, adding that the mutineers were, he thought, cooling down. On this the Rao resolved to go to them himself, and happily succeeded in persuading them to depart with such plunder as they had already obtained. De Kantzow now joined the party at the bridge, and they went to the office, where they found the treasury still secure. Mr. Power explains that he had held the bridge long enough to keep back the bad characters of the "city" (as it is the Anglo-Indian fashion to speak of all chief towns), and that when the sepoys were known to have departed, the urban population at once calmed down.

On the 23rd came more bad news; and Power, by sanction of Government, raised a troop of horse for the maintenance of order, which was commanded by Lieutenant de Kantzow. The magistrate himself took up his post in the "Kutcherry," or office-building, which he fortified by the aid of some sergeants serving in the Department of Public Works. One feature of the defence is too extraordinary to be left out of this record. The Chief Court of the North-West Provinces was then called "The Sudder," and the Sudder had lately issued strict circular orders to all district judges and magistrates for the preparation and maintenance of the records of cases, upon a plan which some of those local officials considered pedantic and troublesome. In the height of the excitement (only two days, in fact, after the terrible morning above described), Mr. Power found himself unable to avoid a triumphant celebration of the "base uses" to which these records had come at last. These are his words:—

"All the Faujdári records" (those of criminal trials) "have been taken up to the roof of the Kutcherry, and being placed behind its railing form an excellent breastwork. This matter had better be reported to the Sudder; but at the same time it may be mentioned that the record-room has undergone a thorough purification by the purpose to which its contents have been applied. I may also mention, for the Court's information, that a good, stout *Khānajangi misl*" (record of an affray case) "*prepared after the Court's latest rules and thickened with false evidence*, is an excellent article of defence; and has, by experiment, been found to be bullet-proof."

The italics are the present writer's. They serve to show an irrepressible *fronde* wielded by a gallant spirit at a time when surely few would have indulged in professional sarcasm.

In this gloomy sanctuary, with perjury imployed as a protection in the most unexpected and unusual fashion, the two brave magistrates and the doctor,* with two or three military officers (they had been joined by Major Hayes † and Captain Carey, Lieutenant Barber and Mr. Fayrer, who brought with them some of the Oudh Irregular Cavalry), held their own for some considerable time. The troopers were posted under Barber and Fayrer at Bhaungaon, where the road from Mainpuri falls into the grand trunk road leading to Cawnpore and Calcutta, and on the 1st June Hayes and Carey started to join them. The troopers had proceeded up the road to Karaoli, and there the officers found them, drawn up in parade order. But the native officers advanced, and warned them that treachery was intended. Hayes and Carey turned their horses' heads back, and rode in the direction by which they had arrived. The troopers spread over the plain in pursuit. Hayes was overtaken, and fell dead

* Messrs. Cocks and Kellner had gone to Agra, where the former soon found other fields of usefulness, as already described.

† He was Secretary to the Oudh Government, and an ardent student. His valuable library perished in the Residency.

with a sabre-cut over the head; Carey, a lighter weight, escaped, and got safely back to Mainpuri; Barber and Fayrer were murdered about the same time at Karaoli; but the worthy lord of the manor, Lachman Singh (afterwards ennobled by Government), rescued all three of the bodies, and taking them to Mainpuri, delivered them to Mr. Power, who duly buried them in consecrated ground.

The rascally troopers departed to Lucknow, where they doubtless took part in the siege. Their place was taken by seventy sabres of the Gwalior Contingent (1st Cavalry), under Major Raikes, who accepted the services of the hard-riding Carey as his second in command. A few Sikh sepoys from disbanded corps, and about a dozen faithful sepoys of the mutinous 9th who had remained faithful to de Kantzow, formed the infantry nucleus. A telegraph-office was opened, and a couple of European refugees were brought in. The local horse, under de Kantzow, amounted to 100 sabres, with three native officers who had left various cavalry corps to come to their homes at Mainpuri on furlough. With these forces the town and station were patrolled, and some insurgent villages punished. Early in June they fought a severe engagement with a strong party of rebels at Bhaungaon; the rebels beat them off, and killed the Thánadar, or native sub-inspector of police, who died bravely in the defence of his post. In this action de Kantzow was severely wounded. An unfortunate turnpike-keeper was about the same time murdered on the trunk road. All the neighbouring districts were now lost, and Mainpuri was nothing more than an imperfect oasis of partial order in the midst of a political wilderness. The trunk road swarmed with mutineers, and the Raja of Mainpuri, whose kinsman had behaved so well on the 23rd May, was known to be planning a treacherous outbreak. The district got rapidly out of hand, some of the sub-collectors and police-officers fled, others joined the rebellion, but honourable exceptions were duly noted. Among these last were both Muhamadans and Hindus, the subordinate judge, the *Kotwál* (head police officer), the deputy collector, and, chief of all, Raja Lachman Singh of Karaoli—a charming old man, whom to know was to love—by whose good-will and vigilance authority was maintained in the teeth of almost overwhelming difficulties and dangers, and the march of mutineers constantly impeded by the abandonment of villages and absence of supplies; other landholders, here and there, evinced the same spirit, and it is indeed creditable to the Indian character that when such men were faithful it was in no ordinary measure, life and wealth being freely hazarded in the cause of the alien Government.

So wore on the month of June, the worst of that bad year. The end was drawing nigh, when no prospect was apparent but a desperate attempt at escape, with the alternative of a soldier's death, or a long uncertain ride through deadly heat to a doubtful refuge. On the 28th the approach of the Jhánsi mutineers, two regiments out of the entire brigade, was announced, and on the 29th their advanced guard reached Mainpuri, where they were joined by the Raja's people and by most of Power's police and levies. They threw open the jail and commenced a regular plunder of the place; and now the last decision had to be taken. Formally consigning the responsibility for Government property to the Raja and Bhawáni Singh, Mr. Power marched out, accompanied by Raikes, Carey, and half-a-dozen other Englishmen, escorted by the Gwalior cavalry, and preceded by Watson, de Kantzow, and James Power. The Gwalior men deserted peaceably on the road, the rest of the party arrived in safety at Agra and joined the refugees in the fort. The district was recovered about the beginning of 1858, and order was without difficulty restored.

We next come to the district of Etáwa, and meet with increasing peculiarities. The land lies upon the Jumna, on whose banks the "city," or chief town, is situated. The ravines have, from of old, been haunted by tribes of semi-savages, called Ahirs, whose criminal propensities are with difficulty restrained even in times of the profoundest peace.* In the uplands a mixed population prevails, though the larger estates are held by Rajput colonists who have been settled there for many generations. The Jumna runs through the whole district, having the Chumbal as a parallel as far as Etáwa. The population at the time was about 365 to the square mile, about one in five being Musalmans. The area is 1,698 square miles.

The magistrate at the time of the outbreak was a man of singular character. Hitherto we have had to describe the deeds of men of the old type of the Company's civil officers, born of the patrician or equestrian orders, brought up in the old unscientific public-school fashion, with no desire for display, doing and enduring what fell in their way with the cheerful stoicism of their class, and narrating their adventures with artless simplicity as if performing the last and least agreeable portion of an unpleasant task.

Mr. Allan Octavian Hume was not altogether a man of that kind, if indeed his peculiar character can be brought into any class at all. A younger son of the late Joseph Hume—that prosperous and energetic surgeon who died, after a long and useful career of public service in 1858, amid the general respect and regret of his countrymen—Mr. Hume had entered the service about eight years before the Mutiny. Quickly distinguished by his activity and acuteness, he had obtained the first great prize of the service—the charge of a district—in an unusually short space of time, and had been selected for what was deemed a post of special difficulty, as magistrate and collector of Etáwa. His qualities are reflected in his official *Narrative*. Though he was absent during the greater part of fifty-seven,† and though order was not restored till the end of

* In or about 1848 these people murdered an English traveller whom they mistook for Mr. Unwin, a magistrate who had offended them in the discharge of his duty.

† The narrative is dated November 18th, 1858, and states in the opening paragraphs that the district contains "here and there bands of rebels too desperate or too blood-stained to listen to our gracious Queen's late message of mercy." This was a year after order had been restored in many of the neighbouring districts.

the following year, he contrived to give his report—written, as he assures us, in twenty-four hours—the air of a chapter of history composed in the style of the late Sir A. Alison. As we shall presently see, however, the abnormal prolongation of disorder in Etáwa was not Mr. Hume's fault; and in courage and initiative he showed himself no unworthy colleague of the Dunlops, Spankies, and others, whenever he was able to command the due amount of force. But it is a drawback to his report that it takes a triumphant tone where most men in the same position would either have said nothing, or would have been content with a more "apologetic" treatment, to use the word in its classical rather than its social sense.

The early abandonment of Etáwa was due, in part at least, to the same cause that led to the evacuation of Mainpuri. Here also was a detachment of the faithless 9th Native Infantry, and here, even earlier than in Mainpuri, the approach of the Jhánsi mutineers made itself felt. Mr. Hume's hands were apparently, but only apparently, strengthened by the arrival of the Grenadier Regiment of the Gwalior Contingent, by whose aid he was enabled to return to his station for a few days, after being driven out by the first outbreak. The ladies were wisely sent into Agra, and with the aid of an excellent native subordinate (still in the service), named Kunwar Lachman Singh, Mr. Hume kept order, as best he could, until the middle of June. But on the 16th of that month the news arrived that the Gwalior Contingent had mutinied and driven the Christians from Gwalior. No further dependence was to be placed on the grenadiers, who plotted treason within earshot of their commandant. Major Hennessey's record of the conversation—so far as was overheard by him that night—deserves record as a specimen of the sort of feelings that were then being disseminated by agitators:—

Whispered conversation took place, of which the following caught my ear: "What is this that has happened at Gwalior?"

"They have given themselves a bad name."

"True," said the emissary; "but all the world knows that for the last three or four years the *Faringhis* have exercised great oppression; they have ruined, and taken the lands of, all respectable Zemindars and given them to *Banias* (mercantile men). It is time to get rid of them. There is no *Izzat* (*prestige*) about their system; they will neither make an Emperor themselves nor allow anyone else to be Emperor: now, too, they attempt to destroy our religion."*

Thus warned, and aware that the Jhánsi mutineers were within two days' march, the British officers departed, taking up on the road some fugitives from Kalpi and Jalaun, of whom two were ladies. Detaching the faithful Lachman Singh to maintain order, and writing to all landholders in whom he confided, Mr. Hume took his post at Agra, where he served with the right half-battery in the action at Sucheta, and was not able to return to his district till the end of December. This must have been felt by him as a severe misfortune; but it hardly warrants the claims to exceptional loyalty on behalf of his district which pervades the pages of his *Narrative*. Constant disturbance prevailed, though several of Mr. Hume's native friends behaved with creditable spirit; and even when he got back on the 30th of December, he found one Rup Singh, and other "refractory Zemindars," at the head of large forces, and rendering his position, as he himself says, "a *very* critical one." He seems to have acted with vigour. Before the end of January he had raised a respectable force, with which, "strengthened by a detachment of Alexander's Horse," he took the field on the 7th of February, and fought a successful action near Anantram, on the Kalpi road, in which it was believed that the rebels lost 150 men. A month later the Rája of Ruru, a rebel leader, lost heart and committed suicide. But the forces of Rup Singh remained in possession of a whole Pargana (subdivision), having a bridge of boats in their rear, by which reinforcements and supplies were constantly reaching them from the other side of the Jumna. The Western tract, spoken of by Mr. Hume as the Jumna-Chambal Duáb, was held by Rája Khushál Singh and his son, who remained in defiant occupation till September.

Mr. Hume's narrative now, and for nearly twelve months

* *District Narrative*, App. V.

more, is little but a record of fighting; and certainly no officer of his cloth saw more purely military service. It is clear, however, from his own admissions that for a long time he neither collected revenue nor exercised any other species of authority much beyond the limits of his own camp. Thus, at p. 13 he says: "Soon after the outbreak I, on my own responsibility, suspended the Government demand." And elsewhere he records that, up to March 1858, he "had collected no money but what was required for immediate use"; and even then it was only "the Zemindars of Bhartna and Etáwa," who "were directed to pay up the revenue." In a third paragraph he states that "care was taken to do nothing, and [to] issue no order in regard to any not openly against us, calculated to provoke opposition or disobedience." He was about this time joined by a column under Colonel Riddell—composition and strength not given.

Great contention raged in and round a village, or town, called Ajitmal, a few miles south of Anantram, in the neighbourhood of which Rup Singh was maintaining disorder. On the 16th March the rebels attacked and plundered Phaphund—near to which is now a station of the East Indian Railway—and on the 30th Mr. Hume felt himself strong enough to move against them in view of chastisement. Driving them out of Ajitmal, he chased them into the ravines of the Jumna, a trifling loss occurring on either side. All this time Kalpi was the head-quarters of a large body of mutineers, and Rup Singh, obtaining reinforcements from thence, surrounded Mr. Hume on the 11th April, and drove him back towards Etáwa. General disorganisation ensued, only partially arrested by a renewed attack on the 21st. The levies then moved on to the river—horse, foot, and artillery—and seized the ferry-boat, inflicting some loss on the retreating enemy. In all these skirmishes Mr. Hume seems to have acted with great personal courage, ably seconded by Mr. Maconochie, his deputy, and Mr. C. Doyle, who had joined him from Meerut after Dunlop's Volunteers—with whom he served there—had been broken up. Lieutenant Furnell, another volunteer, who had been in practice at Mussoorie as a dentist, but was given a local commission for his military services in the Meerut district, also displayed signal gallantry. Both, indeed, were subsequently killed in action. The name of Mr. Furnell does not occur in Mr. Hume's *Narrative*, which makes it the more necessary to record it here: especially should it be noted for the chivalry of his death. When lying mortally wounded, this heroic young man—not a professional soldier, be it remembered—showed only one anxiety, and that was as to the prospect of his associate, Lieutenant Chapman, obtaining the Victoria Cross.

Operations on a more conspicuous scale were at hand. In the beginning of April, Sir Hugh Rose* had taken Jhánsi, and devoted the rest of the month to resting his troops, and preparing them for the advance upon Kalpi, where were collected almost all the remaining leaders of the revolt: the Ráni of Jhánsi, Tantia Topi, and the Nana's brother. The banner of the Peshwa now floated over the last stronghold of rebellion; and Rose, with an army decimated by disease and death in battle, had to move in the terrible summer of those regions in order to remove the last barrier that restrained communica- between Central India and the main army under Lord Clyde. On the 5th May he had advanced within ten miles of Kalpi; on the 19th, being joined by Colonel Maxwell with the Connaught Rangers, the Camel Corps, and some companies of Sikhs, Rose felt strong enough to attack the place. On the following day, after a hard-fought battle, the town was evacuated, and Her Majesty's birthday was celebrated in the last and lost fortress of the rebellion among the trophies of the previous day's victory. Tantia and the Ráni doubled back on Gwalior—with what result is known to all readers of Malleson—but a large body of the rebels crossed the Duáb in search of an asylum in the still-disturbed province of Oudh.

These events kept the Etáwa district—especially the portion

* Now (1883) Field-Marshal Lord Strathnairn, G.C.S.I.

of it washed by the Jumna—in turmoil during the greater part of May and June, and large bodies of mutineers passed whom Colonel Riddell did not feel strong enough to attack. On the 2nd July Mr. Hume was forced by ill-health to make over charge of the district to Mr. G. E. Lance, command of the local levies being assumed by Lieutenant L. Forbes of the 2nd Native Infantry. Rup Singh once more crossed the Jumna, and totally destroyed the unfortunate town of Ajítmal on the 6th. Two days later Mr. Lance, with a force consisting of 200 bayonets, 120 sabres, and 5 guns, drove them out of the ruins, and back into the ravines. This sort of work went on, slow but sure, for the next two months. On the 6th September, the last focus of disorder fell—a place called Chakarnagar—and the last fight (with one exception), took place at Parli on the 23rd October, when some of the forces of the indefatigable Rup Singh were defeated by the local levies under Lieutenant Allen, with the loss of over thirty men, the whole of their ammunition, baggage, and means of transport.

Order having been, as he hoped, finally restored, Mr. Hume —who had resumed charge of his district—wrote the *Narrative*, to which we have mainly owed our information. After making mention of those who had been his chief subordinates and supporters, he proceeds to devote a few paragraphs to various details of his administration during the trying times just passed. As to finance, he explains the reason of his having left the revenue uncollected. He shrewdly remarks that, having lost five lakhs of rupees by the plunder of his treasuries, he judged that the revenue would, just then, be "safer in the hands of a thousand landholders than in a treasury guarded by sepoys too likely to mutiny." When he set himself in earnest to the business of collection, he succeeded in realising the large sum of over twelve lakhs, and the balance was left to be recovered hereafter. He had the satisfaction of reporting that in many places the village-schools had been kept open; that "the little lads were everywhere humming away at their lessons"; and that, when he wrote, there were 179 schools open with an attendance of nearly four thousand scholars. The remainder of the report is devoted to an examination of the causes to which the exceptional loyalty of his district was to be attributed. There is also a brief account of the method by which the villages were led to "submit to arbitration the adjustment of the cost of their transgressions." Of these "*panchaiat* cases," Mr. Hume informs us there were 526, "some of which included the whole of the inhabitants of one or more villages." If one of these statements should seem to militate against the other, there can be at least no doubt but that Mr. Hume surmounted his difficulties—whatever they were—with tact, humanity, and resolution.

His greatest trial was yet to come. His report is dated November 18th, 1858. Three weeks later the district was invaded by Firoz Sháh, a member of the late royal family of Dehli, and the only one who displayed courage and conduct. Escaping southwards from Lord Clyde when the Oudh Begam, the Nana, and some other leaders fled into Nepal, the heroic prince, whose hands were free from innocent blood, and who might have secured a pardon and a pension by simple surrender, preferred to cut his way through the British territories.

On the 6th December vague rumours of the approach of a force, supposed to be headed by the Nana, reached Etáwa, and Mr. Hume immediately took the field, sending information at the same time to the military authorities at Cawnpore on the one side, and Agra on the other. His own force was composed of some 200 infantry, 140 cavalry, 4 guns, and a troop of the Meerut mounted police; the whole under the command of Lieutenant Forbes already mentioned. They marched with the intention of defending a fort called Harchandpur, held by a loyal landholder; and on the morning of the 8th, having driven in the enemy's pickets, found themselves confronted by a fine force of mutinous horse, estimated at 1,400 sabres, with nearly 200 infantry of the 28th Bengal Regiment. The enemy's baggage and transport were guarded by a strong reserve. These men were evidently no unskilled village-rabble, but a body of trained soldiers, whose business was to cut their way through all opposition, or perish in the attempt; and the sequel showed alike their capacity and their resolution. At first, perhaps, surprised, they speedily formed under cover of a village, sending off their baggage towards a bridge crossing the canal. Lieutenant Forbes placing the local horse—under Mr. Doyle—on his right, and the Meerut troop on his left, opened fire from the centre under Messrs. Hume and Maconochie. The enemy, accepting the challenge, advanced so as to outflank the levies, on seeing which Forbes took Doyle's horsemen against the left attack, while the guns played upon the enemy's advance. The charge was only partially successful: Doyle's horse being wounded, the rider fell and was cut to pieces; his men retreated in more or less order. Meanwhile another party of the enemy came down on the English left, but were checked by two successive charges of the Meerut police, ably and bravely led by their Rasaldár, Asadulla Khan. This excellent native officer received a severe wound in the *melée.* But a third body presently got round to the rear, and became engaged with the Etáwa foot. Mr. Hume's position now became very critical; and probably disaster was only averted by the firmness of the remaining foot-soldiers, and the presence of mind of a non-commissioned officer named Edmunds, who was in charge of the largest of the guns. Such clouds of dust were raised by the trampling of the bold and "ubiquitous" horsemen as, added to the smoke from the guns, prevented anything being clearly seen but the constant flash of the flickering sabres. Amid the confusion the levies formed square with commendable coolness, while Edmunds, with "conspicuous address," swung round his 12-pounder gun, and poured grape into the flank of the assailants. The horses were thrown into a state of terror, the men lost heart on seeing the resistance of the square, and the attack ceased after a duration of fully three hours. Each side drew off in good order, and the Etáwa force occupied their original objective—Harchandpur, while the enemy proceeded on their route.

Well might the Governor-General, a man not given to dithyrambics, characterise this as "a daring exploit," and express his "warm commendation of the courage, skill, and determination which marked it." His Excellency gave his thanks to Lieutenant Forbes, to Messrs. Hume and Maconochie, and to Sergeant-Major Edmunds. Doyle's family received a pension, and the brave Rasaldár received a decoration and the title of "Sardár Bahádur." Mr. Hume was deservedly made C.B.

The enemy, who were well mounted and equipped, comprised men of the 1st and 2nd Bengal Light Cavalry, the 11th, 12th, and 13th Irregulars, and a number of unattached rebels and mutineers, many of whom were Afghan and Sikh soldiers of fortune. They lost fifty-eight killed, among whom was the ex-Názim of Farrukhabad—a man who had long sought to disturb the district; many more were wounded, most of whom were duly removed in ambulance "doolies," or litters, with which the rebels were well provided.

The British loss was twenty-one killed and nineteen wounded. Brigadier the Hon. Percy Herbert, coming up from Cawnpore, fell in with some of the fugitives—for such they soon became—and inflicted on them a further loss in material and men; and Brigadier Showers arrived from Agra on the 11th, having marched seventy-five miles in forty hours: he did not, however, succeed in adding to the enemy's loss.

The unfortunate prince probably separated from his men, and eventually—as it is understood—made his way to Mecca. He has never, so far as I am aware, been seen or heard of since.

This was the end of disturbance in the district of Etáwa, which immediately fell into its usual routine. To conclude with the gallant magistrate's fervid words:—

> The tide turned: and then popular goodwill blossomed out and gave fruit in the speedy restoration of peace and order: and now, though here and there

* His futile attempt to co-operate with Tantia Topi is related in Malleson, iv. pp. 359 *et seq.*

blackened and desolate villages and bands of rebels, too desperate or too blood-stained to listen to our gracious Queen's late message of mercy,* remind us of the past, our people are once again quiet and contented, our fields are rich with heavy crops, and we can look forward hopefully to the future, and cheerfully to the labours that shall make that future all, and more, than in the past we ever dreamed of.

Strange, indeed, is the calmness with which the simple folk of Hindustan could plough their land and sow their seed in such times, and the readiness with which they accepted disorder and the restoration of order alike, "with a heart for any fate."

*** On November 1st 1858 the Royal Proclamation, translated into twenty languages, and promulgated throughout the country, announced that Her Majesty had assumed the direct sway of the Indian Empire. So we created a Pádsháh at last!**

CHAPTER V.

CAWNPORE AND FARRUKHABAD.

In this and the next section the treatment must be somewhat different from that adopted hitherto. From Sahâranpur to Etâwa there was no interregnum of pure belligerence; the civil officers being left to deal with the anarchy with such aid as was from time to time available. "Martial law" was generally proclaimed; but the magistracy were, on the whole, the directors of events; and succeeded, in longer or shorter time. In Cawnpore and Farrukhabad, on the contrary, there was a long period when all semblance of authority was obliterated; and the civil officers were scarcely of any weight in affairs, but were mainly restricted to fighting or foraging in association with their comrades of the army, and only gradually employed in restoring order as the tide of war subsided.

Still, in order to complete a civilian's view of the country technically known as "Hindustan"—which was the focus and chief scene of the outbreak—a few circumstances may be noted such as may have escaped the attention of the ordinary historian.

Cawnpore is the chief town of a district, of the same name, lying on the right bank of the Ganges, on the opposite side of which is the province of Audh—or Oude. It was selected as a cantonment so far back as 1777, and formed the basis for the attacks of the British conquerors upon Rohilkand and Dehli. At the time of the outbreak it contained a population of about 100,000, chiefly traders and operatives, in fact the ordinary

Indian urban population. At Bithur—a village some miles higher up the river—lived a Mahratta of rank, named Dhundu Panth, but most commonly known by the title (not unusual among noble Mahrattas) of "Nána Sáhib." He had been adopted in 1832 by the deposed *Peshwa,* Báji Rao, and inherited his private property. But Lord Dalhousie had decided that the titular dignity of Peshwa (head of the Mahratta confederacy) should not pass under the adoption, and the political pension and salute of guns were discontinued on Báji's death in 1852. During the next few years the Nána spent a good deal of money in trying to bring his wrongs before the Queen's Government in England, employing for that purpose a Muslim adventurer named Azimulla Khán, who had been made his private secretary, and who was an accomplished rascal of the Gil Blas, or Casanova, type. While this man was intriguing with third-rate politicians, and philandering with credulous females in Europe, his master shut himself up in his palace at Bithur, where he sulked in splendour, and nursed his wrongs in the society of Baba Bhatt, Bála Rao, and other chosen companions. On stated occasions a British civil officer visited him; and about November there was a religious fair on the river, when refreshments were provided for European visitors. But the Nána never willingly associated, in the slightest degree, with persons of that race from the day on which the Peshwa, his adoptive father, died.

The garrison, at the time of the outbreak, comprised the 2nd Bengal Light Cavalry, a detail of artillery, and three regiments of Bengal Infantry; all the rank and file of which were natives of India. The British troops had fallen below the proportion proper to such a force, a detachment having been sent to the aid of Sir Henry Lawrence at Lucknow. Those that remained at Cawnpore were as follows:—

Artillery—One battery of 6 guns with 59 men;
Infantry—60 men H. M. 84th.
74 invalids H. M. 32nd.
13 1st Madras Fusiliers.

The whole under the command of a distinguished officer of the company's army, Sir Hugh Massey Wheeler, K.C.B. The civil chief was the magistrate and collector, Mr. Hillersdon, of the Bengal Civil Service.

About eighty miles higher up the river was the station of Futtehgarh, the official centre of a district named after the neighbouring city of Farrukhabad. Here was stationed the 10th Native Infantry, a regiment posted there for the protection of the gun-carriage factory in the fort. The civil officer was Mr. W. George Probyn, C.S., the military command being vested in Colonel Smith. After the receipt of the news of the Meerut mutiny, the men of the 10th continued for some time to behave well ostensibly, though in conversation with Mr. Probyn's native informants they admitted that if other sepoys were to attack the Europeans they would not oppose them in arms. All they could guarantee was that they would not kill their own officers. Amid such sinister omens the Europeans prepared for the worst. Messrs. Phillipps and Bramly came in from neighbouring districts, but passed on to Agra where we have already had occasion to notice their services; other refugees afterwards joined, including Mr. W. Edwards, the magistrate of Badaon in Rohilkhand, brother of the R. M. Edwards, mentioned above in connection with the Muzafarnagar district.

Leaving these, to be followed hereafter in a few concise sentences, we return for the present to Cawnpore, where General Wheeler and Mr. Hillersdon were taking counsel as to the best method of weathering the storm until they should receive the assistance that they expected from Calcutta. That city, it should be added, was 628 miles off, only a small portion of the distance being covered by a railway. The people of Cawnpore, therefore, were somewhat in the same situation as that in which the people of Edinburgh had been in 1745.

For what passed at the first we have to trust chiefly to conjecture. But I have been so far fortunate as to obtain the assistance of Mr. J. W. Sherer, C.S.I., who came up with the first relief in July. It is this gentleman's opinion that the steps taken by the civil and military chiefs at this crisis, which led to the disastrous results that have obtained such sad notoriety, were on the whole justified by the circumstances. It is proper to bear in mind that they had peculiar opportunities for forming a forecast. Wheeler was a thorough "sepoy-officer": his habits and associations were those of the old school; he understood, from a life-long experience, the feelings of native troops; he was necessarily in receipt of the most trustworthy information. Hillersdon, for his part, had a brother in command of one of the native regiments; and was, himself, personally intimate with many of the men, among whom the Colonel was a favourite. A month before Colonel Hillersdon told Mr. Sherer—who happened to be on a visit at Cawnpore—that his men had discussed the question of the suspected cartridges, and had declared themselves willing to use them so long as they were permitted to tear off the ends, and were not required to touch them with their teeth. This shows that ticklish topics were not avoided in intercourse with the men. Nor was the Nána openly hostile; on the contrary, Hillersdon is believed to have had reason for hoping that, by promising to obtain the concessions so long pleaded for in vain, he might secure in the Mahratta an influential ally. It is, further, Mr. Sherer's belief that, up to the final outbreak, there was no collusion between the Nána and the sepoys. Whatever communications may have passed between Azimulla and the Court of Dehli—and it is my personal belief that such had been made—the fact that, at the first mutiny, the troops started for Dehli is a proof that they were not then acting with the Bithur people. The British authorities, I repeat, had to provide against tumult arising from the departure of the native troops, and for the safety of the seven or eight hundred Europeans until they could obtain assistance from Calcutta. It was also necessary that the magazine should be guarded, so that the bad characters of the town should not obtain arms. All now seems to point to the conclusion that the cause of the mischief was Azimulla who, on returning from Europe and becoming aware of the discontents of Queen Zinat Mahl at Delhi, thought he saw his way to fame and fortune as a political creator. The Nána was to stand forth as Plenipotentiary of the restored Emperor; though it might be a work of time and trouble to persuade the chiefs of the army to accept this part of the programme. But we ought not to blame Hillersdon for not knowing all this, or for thinking that it was best, in his perplexed situation, to endeavour to outbid the sepoys for the only alliance that had a chance of safety in it. He probably thought, as above suggested, that he could secure the Nána by promising a reconsideration of his case as the reward of his adherence. Only, unhappily, Azimulla had watched the Crimean collapse (see Russell's book on the war, where he mentions having received a visit from the gay rascal in the trenches before Sebastopol). He had also been in correspondence with foes of England on the Continent (the letters and drafts were found at Bithur and fell into the hands of an officer of Bengal Artillery). The Persian war seemed to him a part of the advance of Russia, and he had just enough knowledge of the political drama to be "a dangerous thing," first to Hillersdon, and ultimately to himself and its cause. As will be presently shown, there is evidence that he negotiated with some agents or leaders of the sepoys before they mutinied, though their subsequent march towards Delhi renders it doubtful how far these negotiations had been ratified by the men in general.

Certainly the first events bore out the plans of the British officials. A temporary refuge was secured on the Calcutta side of the town; the troops moved up the Dehli road; the Nána took charge of the magazine. Lastly, since the first batch of the 84th had actually reached Cawnpore from Calcutta, after the news of the Meerut mutiny had been received there, Wheeler was amply justified in expecting timely relief and in communicating his hopes to Hillersdon.

How all turned to sorrow and destruction is known to the readers of Mr. Trevelyan's graphic work, and has been duly chronicled in history. When the troops had reached their encampment on the second stage, the Nána joined them, and succeeded in persuading them that it was not their interest to leave him. The Peshwa had, for some time before the conquest under Lake, represented the Mughal Empire, and carried on (through his Deputy) the administration of Hindustan. It was natural to identify the cause of the Nána, as Peshwa, with the cause being defended at Dehli; largesse and the promise of plunder did the rest. The troops returned to Cawnpore, and joined in attacking the entrenchment.

The conduct of the Nána is an illustration of two truths that must never again be lost sight of in Indian affairs. The first is, that we cannot predict what Asiatics will do on grounds derived from our own notions of what is their duty, or even their interest. The second, that we must put no confidence in those whom we have offended in a deep and enduring manner.

The implacable Mahratta and his confederates declared themselves as foes: the skilful soldier, Tantia Topi; the sleek tiger, Azimulla, fresh from the ill-judged hospitalities of London. On the forenoon of the 7th June, they opened their heaviest batteries on the rude parapets of the entrenchments, so low, that a refugee from the district one day during the subsequent siege entered by leaping his horse over them. For three dreadful weeks the wretched Europeans were sapped, bombarded, starved; but their courage held out. Hillersdon was cut in two by a round shot; his chief subordinate, McKillop, was shot as he was drawing water for the women from an unprotected well; Hillersdon's brother, wife, and two children perished in the fatal *enceinte.* At last came the end. Despairing of succour from Calcutta, and trusting to the promises of the Nána—who offered plausible terms—Wheeler consented to evacuate the scene of horror, and moved out on the 27th to take boat at the Sati Chaura Ghât. What happened there is too well known. The banks of the Ganges were stained with innocent blood. The surviving victims were marched back in captivity, with the exception of one boat's crew, of whom four only finally escaped, two, at least, of whom are still (1883) alive.

In the meanwhile, the Fattehgarh people had gone through somewhat similar sufferings. On the 1st of June they heard of the outbreak at Shajahánpur, where poor Mordaunt Ricketts and his companions were murdered as they were worshipping in church. On the 3rd a party of Audh troops entered the station, and the 10th men fraternised. At 1 A.M. on the 4th some of the white inhabitants, 140 in number, left in boats, hoping to reach Cawnpore, and unacquainted with the state to which matters were tending there. All perished ultimately with a very few exceptions. Colonel Smith, Colonel Goldie, Major Robertson (head of the factory), Majors Munro and Phillott, with some other commissioned and non-commissioned officers, and a number of women and children, remained in the Fort. The fugitives were at first guarded and assisted at Dharmpur by Hardeo Baksh, an Audh landholder, who, indeed, continued faithful to the last to all who continued to avail themselves of his assistance. Of those in the boats, some sought shelter in this gentleman's fortified residence; but Mr. Probyn and two others returned for a time to Fattehgarh. From hence Probyn wrote to Dharmpur, directing that it should be defended to the last, and garrisoned by 500 matchlock-men, for whose pay he would be responsible. On the 10th June he rejoined the party there, accompanied by Mr. W. Edwards and two planters, Messrs. Donald. On the 13th the bulk of the Dharmpur refugees returned to Fattehgarh, on the urgent invitation of Colonel Smith. But Messrs. Probyn and Edwards, with the family of the former, remained in the fort of Hardeo Baksh, as they did not trust the 10th Native Infantry.

On the morning of the 18th their anticipations were fulfilled, The sepoys of the 10th finally abjured their allegiance, placed the descendant of the Muhamadan Nawábs on the throne, divided the contents of the treasury, and disbanded quietly. Only one man remained faithful; his name was Kálé Khán.

The Europeans in the fort now prepared for an attack. This ensued in a few days, being headed by the 41st Native Infantry, who had marched in from Sitápur in Audh. After a brave defence—for which he had only thirty-two men—Colonel Smith evacuated the untenable place by night on the 4th July. Some were killed on the voyage; those who ran the gauntlet reached Bithur or Cawnpore, where they swelled the slaughter there. Only two escaped, Messrs. Churcher and Jones.

The narratives—especially a supplementary one by Mr. C. R. Lindsay, Mr. Probyn's successor—afford harrowing details of some of these incidents; but they have little relation to our subject, and their recapitulation can serve no good purpose. Sufficient to say that great courage was displayed by the unhappy fugitives. On at least one occasion they landed and chased away their pursuers with loss; on another, to avoid the consequences of capture, the non-combatants of one boat leapt overboard, and were drowned or killed in the water. Our countrymen and countrywomen have never been exposed to more dreadful trials, and never underwent trial more valiantly. One who lost friends in those scenes may be pardoned if he declines to dwell upon them. Hardeo Baksh protected Edwards and the Probyns as long as he could, and then sent them down, disguised, by water, and handed them in safety to the British authorities (who had then recovered Cawnpore), on or about the 1st September.

A momentary glance may be allowed on the other side of the Duáb. At Fatehpur, Mr. Sherer, the then magistrate, executed a skilful retreat, and conducted all committed to his charge *viâ* Banda to Mirzápur, whence he himself presently proceeded to the Grand Trunk Road, where he fell in with the avenging force under General Havelock. Robert Tucker, the district judge, insisted on remaining where, indeed, his remaining was worse than useless. He died at Fatehpur, fighting to the last. Mounting to the roof of his court-house, with rifles and ammunition, he defended himself and his records desperately. It is said that some of the assailants got into a tree which commanded the roof, and fired upon him till his arm was broken; they then assumed courage to get on to the roof and cut his throat. Another version, which one would gladly prefer, is that he was shot dead at once. At Hamirpur Messrs. T. K. Loyd and D. Grant, totally defenceless, took refuge in the ravines of the Jumna, where they were followed, and mercilessly shot down like wild animals. Such is the savage state to which the human race is soon reduced when deprived of the restraints of civilisation! *Homo homini lupus.*

We are not without glimpses at civil life in Cawnpore and Farrukhabad during those days of darkness. Whatever good our country may get from India, the good that India will eventually receive in return is more than compensation. But the process is slow. When the strong hand and will of the Imperial race were temporarily paralysed it was soon seen what a poor thing was the civilisation of a people that, having been reduced to anarchy beneath the heel of armed violence for nearly 800 years, had been in leading strings ever since without having learned to walk alone.

Colonel Williams, whom we saw at Meerut, was sent down to Cawnpore after the restoration of order; and he took the evidence of forty-two persons who had been present in June 1857, among whom were Christians, Muhamadans, and Hindus. From these it appeared that the Nána and his brother, called "Bála Sáhib," had tampered with agents of the troops as early as the 1st of the month, assisted by the rascally secretary, though—if Mr. Sherer's surmises be correct—without the troops being pledged to remain at Cawnpore; that the conspirators obtained assistance from several farmers and from the scoundreldom of the bazaars; that 10,000 persons assembled at the fatal ghat to witness the first massacre; and that the chiefs —accompanied by Tantia Topi—sate on carpets upon the estrade before the temple, privileged spectators at the festival of carnage. That, during the second massacre—when, for hours, the women and children of our race were hacked to pieces in the slaughter-house—these wretches sat in a neighbouring hotel looking on at a "nautch"; that all sorts of incompetent ruffians were employed as police officers; and that plunder of the respectable citizens raged unchecked and encouraged. A court, composed of Bába Bhatt, Azimulla, and some pleaders, was formed on the 17th, which sat to hear criminal cases; but the accused were of the humbler classes and the punishments were cruel and capricious. A gypsy had his hand cut off on a charge of theft; some poor men's huts were razed to the ground "for disreputable livelihood." Supplies, extorted by torture, were openly stolen by the officers and men as they came in. On the 1st of July the Nána was solemnly enthroned as Peshwa, and persons were sent into the district to collect revenue; on the 3rd the troops showed signs of disaffection, and were appeased by distribution of pay. The Nána passed most of his time in pleasure at Bithur, till compelled by his followers to show himself and return to Cawnpore. The arrival of Havelock scattered the ruffians, never to meet again; and the British were received by the people with every sign of joy and welcome.

Mr. Sherer, who had—as we saw—joined Havelock on the road after successfully leading his party into a place of temporary safety, assumed some kind of authority at Cawnpore, and at once attempted to form administrative outposts. But the attempt was premature; and after two of his police officers had been killed by the enemy, General Neill directed him to stay further efforts for the present. A military police, under Captain Bruce, of the Bombay army, was organised for the city and immediate neighbourhood, and Mr. Grant (then in charge of the civil administration, and afterwards, as Sir J. P. Grant, the successful governor of Jamaica) sanctioned these measures, which were deemed necessary on military grounds, to which just then all was necessarily subordinated. Bruce was an able and energetic man, and Sherer gave him full and willing co-operation, confining himself to transit and commissariat work, in which he was admirably seconded by a Brahmin Tahseeldar named Bholanáth, whom he had known at Fatehpur.

An idea, however, arose—as ideas will rise in times of general excitement—that Mr. Grant and his civil subordinates resented General Neill's arrangements; and this got so much credit in England, that the late Charles Dickens was led to embody it in a tale in *Household Words*, in which much sport was made of the pompous obstructiveness of "Mr. Commissioner Pordage." Like most things of the sort, it was short-lived, and I believe the tale has dropped—as it was only proper that it should—out of all collections of Mr. Dickens's works. Neither at Cawnpore nor anywhere else did Mr. Grant obstruct any good work; nor is it needful that this statement should be made, were it not that the calm wisdom of that really distinguished official is not so generally recognised as might have been the case had he possessed the love of display and advertising power that are sometimes found in public men. Mr. Sherer well remembers referring to him about some temporary difficulty about the use of the telegraph, and receiving Mr. Grant's answer: "Whatever you do, give no offence to the military authorities." On another occasion, the late Sir James Outram—one of Britain's truest heroes—wrote to the same officer: "So far from taking offence, or relaxing your endeavours to aid us, you ever exerted your utmost influence in the district, with the most unwearied, unceasing personal labours in our behalf. Your hearty, cordial good-will and friendly assistance were deeply felt by us all."

This much upon an uninviting subject. Neill and Sherer and Bruce all worked thoroughly in concert, and there was never the least misunderstanding between red-coats and black-coats.

After Havelock's arrival, the farmers began to negociate about payment of land-revenue; but, of course, the money was the only proof of their sincerity, and much had yet to be done and endured before much of that demonstration could be achieved. It became clear soon that Cawnpore was only a military post, and that the troops collected there were not immediately intended for the pacification of the Duáb, but for more remote purposes. The new-born desire to conciliate subsided; men turned to Gwalior for a new dawn of disorder which had more promise of permanence. The best of the Rajput clans and their leaders were not more than neutral. When Sir James Outram arrived, reorganisation proceeded more rapidly; then came the certainty of the fall of Dehli, and renewed offers of money, but not much actual payment. Some native gentlemen undertook the duty of temporary tahsildárs (sub-collectors), but their want of business habits crippled their efficiency; still, it was felt to be a beginning. The tracts bordering on the Jumna (where Gwalior influences were strongest) continued in open rebellion; even at Bithur a number of Bruce's police were surprised and slaughtered at the great November festival of the *Dasahra*. The fall of Dehli again filled all the tracts bordering on the Trunk road with a demoralised soldiery; but Greathed's column cleared the way. Then the commander-in-chief crossed the Ganges and proceeded to relieve Lucknow; Cawnpore was left to the protection of General Windham's small force; and the Gwalior contingent at length arrived and delivered the most successful attack that was made by any of the enemy during the whole war. When Sir Colin returned, on the 28th November, his first care was naturally the safe departure of the rescued women and children from Lucknow; the force under Windham was then cooped up in the entrenchment, the whole town being in the enemy's hands. On the 1st December, Captain Bruce made over charge to Sherer, the two despatching their business in a house which was being raked by round shot. But the triumph of the mistaken mutineers was soon lost. As soon as Sir Colin heard of the safe arrival at Allahabad of the precious convoy he had done so much to rescue, he turned fiercely upon the enemy, whom he chased from the district before proceeding to relieve Farrukhabad.

At that place, as we have already seen, power had been conferred by the mutineers upon a titular Nawáb who lived there on a pension, being, in fact, the lineal representative of a Rohilla family who had usurped power there during the decline of the

Mughal Empire. Towards the end of June the mutineers inaugurated his reign by the massacre of a score of Christian captives who had survived the previous troubles. The day was rainy, but the spectacle attracted a large crowd to the parade-ground where it took place. The district was then made into two grand divisions, the east and west, each being placed under Názims, or commissioners, one of whom was an imbecile drunkard, the other a ruthless tyrant. There was also a court of two (*military officers*), for the hearing of appellate causes; under these were Muftis, or Judges, men who had formerly held subordinate posts in the British administration. The Nawáb himself was a man of quiet character, much absorbed in the fine arts, as understood by him; and his insignificance was recognised after the return of the British, when his life was spared on condition of his retiring permanently to Mecca. His share in the administration was confined to the promulgation of rules, borrowed from the British, for the administration of justice and the collection of the revenue. On paper the rules look fair enough, therefore; but Mr. Lindsay got together abundant proof that they had but little effect in practice. "Each man ruled as he liked; the Tahsildárs became nonentities; there was much writing, as in our courts; in lieu of stamp-papers, fees were levied. Some of the decisions are curious enough; in one case a Hindu murderer was released on promising to become a Muhamadan. In a case of rape, the defendant was fined two rupees and dismissed." The following is a precept addressed to a police officer in a murder-case:—

"You are directed to go in person to the village, and collecting fifty of the most respectable inhabitants, write their depositions in the following manner: 'We have not killed the deceased, nor are we aware who were the murderers.' . . . But, if they know who the criminals are, you shall write their depositions thus: 'We have not killed the deceased, but certain other persons have. We say this by our faith and on our oath.' And, when taking these depositions, you must administer the oath in the following manner: 'We swear by the Almighty God, who made us and the universe.'"

It does not appear that any result ensued on this strange proceeding, which only shows the childish imitativeness of people who have observed forms without discovering their principle. The sentences, however, were sometimes very severe: the penalty for theft was amputation of the right hand; in a case of undoubted murder the sentence was that the culprit was to give up his property to the complainant, or to be killed by him; on the failure of either of these alternatives, he was to be blown away from a gun. The slaughter of oxen was prohibited, they were not even to bear burdens; this, being, of course, a concession to the Hindu sepoys. A system of barrier-dues was imposed in the town, the proceeds of which, together with the excise, went to the privy purse of the Nawáb. Most articles bore an *ad valorem* duty, which in some cases reached a rate of seven per cent. Prices were trebled, and the trade in piece-goods became a monopoly. On one occasion the proceeds of the Farrukhabad octroi rose to 1,700 Rs. in one day. Similar duties were raised in outlying towns, the proceeds being realised by the sepoys. Civil war went on from time to time, and one of the Názims—the drunkard—received a wound and lost his influence, which had been founded on a belief that he was invulnerable. Farrukhábad continued for seven months to be a centre to which unsuccessful leaders repaired from time to time as they were beaten out of other places. At length this place had to take its turn, too. In the end of December Sir Colin appeared upon the scene. The Nawáb fled on the 2nd January 1858, accompanied by Firuz Sháh and another of the Dehli princes who had joined him; next day British authority was restored on the Western side of the Ganges. About the 18th, Brigadier Adrian Hope won a battle over the rebels at Shamsábád, and the enemy sustained a final defeat at the hands of Sir T. Seaton on the 7th April at Bangaon. After May, order was rapidly and permanently restored.

In the Cawnpore district the progress of events was necessarily somewhat different. The apparent ebb and flow of British success, already noticed, continued for some time to puzzle the waiters on events. There was no enthusiasm felt for the Nána, who was soon seen to be a mere obese voluptuary with no talent for affairs and no courage in the field. But there was, among the humbler classes, a revival of the lawless element that had come down in the blood from the great anarchy of the last century—a factor never to be overlooked in the social questions of Hindustán. There was also a revival of old clan-feeling, the pleasure of foray and reprisal, unclouded by the fear of the police, or the shadow of the tax-gatherer. The people were out for a holiday, and enjoyed it like badly-taught school-boys. Lastly, the dread that the return of British power would be accompanied by the return of the auction-purchaser—an evil, perhaps necessary, and which must apparently cling to a civilisation whose resources come from land-revenue—enlisted many interests against the cause of order. Bacon long ago remarked:—"It is certain, so many overthrown estates so many votes for troubles."*

But after the final reduction of the great rebel stronghold at Lucknow in the spring of 1858, all began to cool down. The southern *parganas* (hundreds) continued to feel the effect of the long disorders in Central India. But then came Sir Hugh Rose's victory at Kalpi, referred to in treating of Etáwa. Temporary distraction was caused by Prince Firoz's last appearance; but it was only temporary. By the winter the district was entirely reoccupied and composed. Mr. Sherer's printed narrative is dated 13th January 1859; and it concludes with a pleasing picture:—

> I followed but the other day close upon the retreating footsteps of Feroze Shah; but I found the ploughman in the field, the boy singing at the well as he urged the bullocks down the slope, the old woman sitting at her door twisting her little cotton-gin, and her daughters grinding millet; all supremely unconscious of the descendant of Timoor, who with unseemly haste had made but yesterday a royal progress through their village.

* Sherer's *Narrative*, p. 16.

One more subject connected with the civil administration of Cawnpore deserves at least a passing notice. In an earlier chapter a story told in Mr. Bosworth Smith's *Life of Lawrence*, was quoted as an illustration of the difficulties that attended the efforts of the civil officers to prevent hasty reprisals at the expense of more or less innocent natives of India. As such the anecdote may pass; but as an incident of life at Cawnpore, it is neither correct nor well-fancied. The "Mess" at Cawnpore consisted of men like Frederick Gubbins, Sherer, Power, Mowbray Thomson, Dr. Tresidder, Martin, and others, with Inglis, W. H. Russell (of *The Times*), Layard, Grenfell, &c. for guests, none of whom were likely to "insult" Mr. Batten on account of due or undue leniency had he wished to show it, or had the power of doing so. In fact, I believe Mr. Batten had very little voice in the earlier part of the administration; and those who had were for the most part successful and efficient enough to be independent of harsh procedure. As soon as the revenue was collected at all, it came in without need for coercive measures. A fine was imposed upon the city, which was promptly paid, with one unsuccessful protest conducted by an English solicitor. Neither during the rebellion nor afterwards was a single sepoy blown from guns at Cawnpore. Four or five officers held special commissions, and persons accused of crimes were tried by them, of whom some were properly executed, others acquitted; the sentences being invariably reported to the Government. General Neill's melodrama, of making the people clean the slaughter-house, was played once and then withdrawn, two persons in all being made to take part in it. Comparing the conduct of the authorities at Cawnpore with the reprisals of most conquerors—even with those of others in the like situation at the time in other parts of India—the recovery of power there was marked by a most singular and creditable moderation.

CHAPTER VI.

BANDA AND ALLAHABAD.

The Allahabad "Division"—of which the district of Cawnpore is a constituent—forms the eastern extremity of the famous Duáb with which we have hitherto been concerned. In addition to Cawnpore the other sections are the districts of Fatehpur, Hamirpur, Banda, and Allahabad. Regarding the two former there is no more to be said than what has incidentally come before us in looking at Cawnpore. Banda and Allahabad, however, will furnish illustrations of some characteristics of the outbreak, though (principally from want of literary ambition on the part of the narrators) the material is not all that could be desired.

The district of Banda contains a little over three thousand square miles, and the population, at the time of the outbreak, may have been something more than half a million, chiefly Ráj-puts of more or less pure blood. As in the rest of Bundelkhand (to which, from a scientific point of view, it belongs) the physical properties of the soil have had a good deal to do with the state of the people. Studded with isolated rocks, interspersed among tracts of dry basaltic black soil, it is unfertile unless irrigated, and when irrigated peculiarly unwholesome. In the Banda district there are few large estates or rich landholders; but at the chief town there resided, in 1857, a mediatised prince, the Nawáb Ali Bahádur, representative of a bastard family of

Mahratta origin who had usurped power there in the anarchy of the last century, and had embraced the creed of Islám. The town stands on the right bank of the river Kén, an important affluent of the Jumna, and is about ninety-five miles south-west of Allahabad.

At the time of the outbreak the chief civil officer was Mr. F. O. Mayne, who—in spite of his friendly *sobriquet* of "Foggy" —was a man who exercised considerable personal influence over those with whom he came in contact. Any defect of insight or scholastic culture was more than compensated by rectitude and energy; the power to see the duty nearest to his hand, the will to carry it out. He died some years ago; a handsome building at Allahabad testifies to the respect and regard of his comrades and subordinates. It is to this gentleman's *Narrative* that we are chiefly indebted for the sketch that follows.

Shortly after receiving news of the disasters at Dehli and Meerut, Mr. Mayne found it necessary to strengthen his police force at out-lying stations, and to put an embargo on the ferries of the Jumna by which persons of a dangerous character might otherwise pass into his territory and stir up a rebellious spirit among the people. The roads were patrolled by horsemen, and strong posts stationed at all the approaches to the town. The English officers personally visited the town police-posts by night, and some of the native gentry and traders were allowed to entertain armed men for their own protection. Help was also obtained from the chief of Ajigarh and other places in the neighbourhood; and these measures were for some time efficacious in maintaining tranquillity. The regular troops consisted of three companies of the 1st Native Infantry, commanded by Lieutenant Bennett.

But the elements of disaster were too strong. First, there was the depressed condition of the people of the district, "ruined"—it is the Magistrate and Collector who says so— "by over-assessment and . . . half-starving." Then came proclamations issued by the British authorities at Agra, apparently without Mr. Mayne's consent. Released convicts from the broken jails of the neighbouring districts soon poured in, confirming and exaggerating the news of trouble elsewhere. The first outbreak in the district was not a military mutiny but a rural rising; a Tahsili (Sub-Collector's office) was sacked, and the records were destroyed by the villagers, "in order (as they said) that no record of their liabilities might remain to the new government." The process was repeated in other quarters; and Mayne saw the tide of rebellion rising rapidly all round him as he sate at his solitary post at Banda; his deputy, Mr. Cockerell, holding a still more lonely watch at the head-quarters of the sub-division of Kirwi. The native officials, generally, showed much staunchness, remaining at their posts as long as they could do any good by remaining; not a few being killed or wounded in the defence of Government property. Still, it is plain that there was not in Banda that backbone of popular energy and good-will which existed in some districts and which enabled Dunlop, for example, to make such short work with revolt in Meerut. A warning against the too frequent practice of treating unpleasant districts as penal settlements for unsuccessful or disfavoured officers, a practice to which was probably attributable the depressed condition of the Banda peasantry. On rare occasions—as in Mayne's own case—a distinguished officer would be sent to a place like this, being promoted for the purpose before his time; but usually the other course is believed to have been adopted. Men who were not esteemed by "Government" were deputed to these stations; feeling themselves discredited and ill-used, they worked sulkily and without zeal; and the people, as of old, suffered for the folly of their rulers, and bore them no affection.

Nor was the condition of the town itself much more assuring. Mutinous talk was heard among the sepoys, though as a body they were still trusted; Mayne even went the length of sending much of his treasure to other districts under guards of these men, and confiding the balance to the care of the detachment, in whose lines he deposited the specie. An attempt was made to fortify the jail as a place of refuge, but this had to be subsequently abandoned on sanitary grounds.

On the morning of the 8th June, as Mr. Mayne was sitting in his office, word was brought that a body of horse was approaching the bridge of boats at Chilatára on the Jumna. An *émeute* in the town took place at once and plundering commenced. The police were employed with effect, and the ladies were removed into the Nawáb's palace. In the meanwhile it was discovered that the supposed invaders were in truth the English refugees from Fatehpur, conducted by Mr. Sherer; and this party arrived in Banda the same evening. But unfortunately the native officer stationed at the bridge had thought fit to accompany them; the road being thus left open, bands of rebels followed, and general demoralisation was soon displayed.

The ladies therefore remained in the palace, which was guarded by some of the English gentlemen, while others—among whom Sherer was conspicuous—took part in patrolling the town. On the night of the 12th, in spite of these precautions, two bungalows were burned, and the English began to make the palace defensible. Whatever they could do against outward enemies they seem to have done; unhappily some, at least, of their foes were of their own household.

On the 14th the detachment of the 1st received news of the mutiny of the regiment at Cawnpore. The 53rd broke out on the same day at the neighbouring station of Hamirpur and murdered the Christians at that station. Bennett reported his men as being utterly beyond control, and was accordingly put in command of a small body of the Nawáb's men, with whose aid Mayne proposed to disarm the men of the 1st and make them give up the ammunition and treasure in their possession. Bennett showed the utmost coolness and resolution; the Nawáb wavered and vacillated for awhile, but was kept up to the mark by Mayne. The attack, however, proved a failure; Bennett's subalterns, Fraser and Clerk, were chased from the parade-ground with jeers, and esteemed fortunate in being able to join the refugees in the palace. All was over, for the time. The detachment was in successful mutiny, joined by the Nawáb's men; and all that was left for Mayne and his associates was to make the best retreat in their power, hampered as they were by the presence of seventeen women and a number of children, for whose safety they were responsible. Mr. H. B. Webster* with a few volunteers clearing the way, they left Banda at 8 o'clock that evening, reaching the friendly fort of Kalinjar at the end of their first march. They had hardly left the town before the station (European) was in a blaze, which lighted them ten miles on their way.

Meanwhile Cockerell had also left his untenable post at Kirwi. On the morning after Mayne's departure (15th June) he rode into Banda, where he was shot down at the gateway of the palace. The refugees reached Mirzápur after a long but unmolested march; and Sherer, proceeding to Allahabad, joined Havelock's advance on Cawnpore, while Mayne remained for the time watching his opportunity to recover his district.

Meantime the Nawáb had endeavoured to take charge, sometimes obeyed, sometimes opposed by the sepoys. All the remaining Christians were gradually hunted down and murdered. The contagion spread rapidly through the district; old scores were paid, auction-purchasers and decree-holders were ousted, caravans were stopped and plundered, the reign of anarchy prevailed as in the old days before the British conquest. "Never was revolution more rapid, never more complete." [Mayne].

The sepoys marched off to Cawnpore on the 19th with the treasure and ammunition; and the Nawáb, relieved by their departure, set to work to form a government, though with a heavy heart, and secret wishes for the return of the British. With them he attempted to open correspondence through Mayne, by whom, however, his letters were not answered. The fort of

* Since the able Inspector-General of Police, N.W.P.

Kalinjar continued to be held by Lieutenant Remington, of the 12th Native Infantry. The rest of the district became more and more a moral wilderness, though imperfect order was maintained in the precincts of the town of Banda, whose citizens were harried by pecuniary requisitions.

About the beginning of April, 1858, the chief's eyes began to be opened to his false position. While he had been doing his best to guard against small bodies of British troops crossing the Jumna, he suddenly heard of the approach of the Madras column from the south-west under General Whitlock. The first action was fought at Kalrai, twenty-four miles from Banda, on the 17th April, when the Nawáb's troops retreated and saved their guns. On the 19th they were again driven off from a nearer field, and pursued up to the banks of the Kén, on which the town of Banda stands: the town itself was occupied without resistance on the following day.

"In a district," says Mr. Mayne, "in which our prestige had suffered so severely, from which we had been nearly a year absent, and where so many different bands of mutineers from time to time had congregated, and where the rebel government had been so long supreme, it was necessary that our return should be accompanied with a force sufficient to make a strong demonstration, to overawe all opposition, and at once to disarm and disperse the disaffected."

Having this requisite, the magistrate resumed his duties on the 29th April, and at once set to work to re-establish his authority. He adds, however, the humiliating confession that the conduct of the British troops was for several weeks far from what was suited to reassure "the frightened and doubting natives." And there were two chiefs still at Kirwi, retaining possession of the eastern half of the district, with 15,000 men and forty pieces of artillery; moreover, tact and judgment were required in restoring order where the whole district had rebelled, and "there was not a village marked in the map that had not, more or less, committed itself." He therefore wisely determined to single out a few of the most guilty in each Pargana, in which alone extreme severity should be exercised; contenting himself with levying pecuniary compensation for the offences committed by the others. A column of demonstration swept the country, being everywhere well received, save in two places which harboured notorious offenders, and where due examples were made. Major Dallas, who commanded this column, was an officer of judgment and intelligence, whose firm yet conciliatory proceedings met with due acknowledgment from the able magistrate. A new police force was organised, the Tahsilis were reopened, and on the 1st June the general proceeded in person to the reduction of Kirwi. At the same time the rebels were driven from Kalpi by Sir Hugh Rose; and the tranquil occupation of the entire district quickly ensued. About four-and-twenty villages that had obtained an evil prominence in crime were burned, and their head men hanged or flogged, while a few more armed demonstrations sufficed for the entire restoration of order. Mr. Mayne modestly attributes this rapid progress to all causes except his own great determination and local knowledge; and he concludes his report with the quaint suggestion that "no greater boon could be bestowed on the North-West Provinces than to dissolve the Regulations and Acts altogether." This *naif* aspiration for the substitution of personal government for the reign of Law was fortunately disregarded; it is only mentioned here as an illustration of the absence of statesman-like insight which is not inseparable from great administrative capacity in the ranks of the Indian Civil Service. The concluding words are alike characteristic of the humanity and of the loyalty of the class:—

"Since closing the report the Queen's proclamation assuming the government of the country has been issued. . . . and all prisoners under trial who came under the amnesty have been released, to the number of upwards of 300 men.

"God save the Queen."

In Book XVII. of his *History of the Indian Mutiny* (Vol. III., p. 399 of the first edition), Colonel Malleson gives some sample sketches of the work of civil officers during the revolt which it has been our present business to study in detail. In speaking of Allahabad, the author mentions, as fully as the proportions of his work allowed, the condition of the town and station; but it will be here necessary to expand those terse and just paragraphs, and to endeavour to give some idea of the events not only there, but in the outlying tracts of which Allahabad was the centre.

The "Division," or Commissionership of Allahabad contains, as already stated, a large tract of country divided into administrative districts, in some of which authority was, for a time, entirely swept away. The district especially named after the city is of considerable extent—the area being 2,765 square miles—and the population is very various, being marked off with some sharpness by geographical limits. The principal rivers are the Jumna and the Ganges, the latter partly flowing within its borders, partly separating it from Mirzapur and Oude. The total number of inhabitants in 1857 was about one million, almost all Hindus; in the Duáb, however, (the portion between the two great rivers,) the estates were largely held by Muslims. Led by them, the people rose in actual rebellion; the Brahmans who lived by the pilgrimages to be presently described took the same line: a man of obscure origin who assumed the title of "Maulvi" (Mollah, or Doctor of Divinity), raised the green flag and preached a crescentade; the district police joined, and general anarchy was for a time established. Beyond the Ganges, so far as it intersects the district, there were other classes and other interests. Here the estates were large and held by Rájput clans, some of whom, ruined by their own mismanagement, had been dispossessed by mortgagees and judgment-creditors; but still maintained their prestige among the cultivating classes, who are believed to have paid them tribute out of which they maintained some degree of comfort and position, supplemented by plunder, even in the quietest times. In the parts south of the Jumna, where neither set of conditions prevailed, three well-affected chiefs preserved some show of order, one of them especially—the Mánda Raja—taking charge of the public treasure and managing the police.

In the town itself great elements of confusion existed. Although, as a Mughal settlement, it was not a place of any but strategic importance, it had preserved traditions of sanctity from the days of Asoka, the contemporary of the ancient Macedonian Empire, whose obelisk still stands in the fort, bearing the celebrated edicts of the reforming monarch. In a grotto close by stands the *Akshai Bat*, representative of the sacred tree of Buddha, watered by subterranean droppings believed by the Hindus to be the reappearance of the Saraswati, "the lost river" of the Sirhind plain, which, according to them, reappears here to join the Jumna and Ganges in their united progress to the sea.

Thus honoured, the "meeting of the waters" has for two thousand years continued, in spite of political, even of religious, revolutions, to be the holiest spot in Hindustan; the "field of bliss," where it is more meritorious to bestow the smallest copper coin in alms than it would be to lavish the largest sums elsewhere. Naturally, such a place would be the hunting-ground of religious mendicants, the scene of some of those bathing-fairs that form, in so many sacred river-sites, the combined resorts of pleasure and piety among the simple folk of Hindustan. As at Hardwúr, Muttra, Benares, so here, numerous gatherings take place on various festal days; while in the pleasant season of Indian winter the plateau between the Jumna and the fort is frequented by a special attendance that collects on an average little less than a quarter of a million of human beings. To minister to the zeal of the pilgrims, to slake their thirst for instruction, and to initiate them into the accurate observance of rite and mystery, a large confraternity of idle friars has been formed whom ignorant Europeans are in the habit of designating by the name of *Fakirs* (borrowed from Muhamadanism), but whose special description is Prágwáls, or "Brothers of the Confluence."

Mention has been made of the fort. The obelisk and grotto point to the conclusion that the place was considered important as far back as the days of the Palibothran Empire. But the present structure dates from A.D. 1575, when the great Mughal monarch, Akbar, was engaged in the final struggle with the *Sharki*, or Eastern, dynasty of Afghan kings. It was then that he saw the advantage of establishing a place of arms at the spot where his dominions in Hindustan were most open to invasion, and whence they could most profitably direct the channel of attack. The old castle has lost much of its mediæval aspect in being adapted to the purposes of modern warfare under its present masters, the British. In the words of Heber, "the lofty towers have been pruned down, the high stone ramparts topped with turf parapets, and obscured by a green sloping glacis." Massive barracks and magazines conceal or even replace the council-halls and seraglios of the Mughals; whose great gateway—still a splendid relic in Heber's days—is now completely masked by the modern stucco-and-brick-work of "the Wellesley-Ravelin."

In the spring of 1857 the garrison comprehended a wing of the Sikh "Regiment of Firozpur," and the 6th Native Infantry; two troops of Irregular Cavalry, under Captain Hardinge and Lieutenant A. Alexander, came in from Partabgarh, by order of Sir H. Lawrence; and—most valuable of all—sixty British artillerymen were sent for from the invalid depôt at Chunar, under command of an old Haileybury man, Lieutenant the Hon. C. J. D. Arbuthnott, who afterwards did excellent service with the levies in Bahár.

The morning of the 6th June dawned in apparent quiet. Some of the white folks had sought safety in the fort, which was garrisoned by the invalided gunners and the Sikhs. These latter were not yet trusted. It was known that men of that class had misconducted themselves at Benares, where indeed a sister regiment had just met with punishment, as will be shown hereafter. It was not known that the Sikh nation, and the people of the Punjab in general, were to make common cause with the British against their old enemies the Hindustanis. It is even stated by Mr. Fendall Thompson, the writer of the official *Narrative*, that the authorities of Allahabad had been warned against trusting their Sikh sepoys by Sir Henry Lawrence himself, the friend of that race. The treasure, therefore, was not entrusted to the Sikhs nor brought into the fort, although one hundred and ten volunteers had been armed from the arsenal and added to the strength of the garrison.

The chiefs of the British administration were Mr. Charles Chester, the Commissioner, and Mr. M. Court, the Magistrate. On the latter devolved, in virtue of his office, the responsibility of not moving the treasure and the whole details of preparation. The day passed on. In the afternoon a parade was held in cantonments for the purpose of reading to the men of the 6th the letter of thanks addressed to them by the Governor-General in Council on their volunteering to march against their insurgent comrades at Dehli. At 8 P.M. the different detachments of the garrison marched to their respective batteries, and sentries posted on the ramparts kept a brisk look-out. They had not long to wait. At 9 o'clock a rocket was seen to rise from the bridge of boats, answered by a similar signal from the lines of the 6th Native Infantry in cantonments. Shortly after firing was heard; and presently a note was brought from Lieutenant Harward, R.A., announcing that the sepoys had carried off two guns, and that he had gone in pursuit with two troops of Irregular Cavalry under Lieutenant Alexander. The rest is well known. Alexander was shot in charging the guns; Harward and others swam the river twice and got into the fort; five officers of the 6th and eight unposted cadets were murdered in or near the mess-house; the jail was thrown open, the station was fired, plunder and slaughter raged; by morning thirty-nine persons of Christian blood had perished.

At the inner main-gate of the fort—near the above-mentioned Wellesley Ravelin—a company of the 6th remained, sympathising perhaps with their comrades outside but afraid to follow their example. These were at once disarmed by the volunteers and expelled from the fort. This measure was ably carried out by Lieutenant Brasyer, of the Sikh Regiment, one of those veterans almost peculiar in those days to the East India Company's service, who had risen from the ranks, and was destined to rise still higher. But it is not my part to dwell on military merit, however conspicuous. I return to my own subject. The disarming being happily accomplished without bloodshed or accident of any sort, the English in the fort began to breathe freely. On the 9th some confusion was caused by the misconduct of some of the volunteers who, being sent to remove stores from the Steam-Agency premises, took to plundering and drunkenness on their own account. But this was not followed by any serious consequences at the moment; and on the 11th Colonel Neill, arriving from Calcutta with forty men, at once assumed command, and began to restore discipline among the volunteers and the Sikhs who had followed the example of disorganisation. In the meantime the mutineers of the 6th Native Infantry had crossed the river with their plunder; but they had thrown away their arms for greater convenience in carrying bags of specie, and as soon as they crossed the river they were set upon by the villagers and spoiled of their ill-gotten gains. Disarmed and demoralised, they dispersed and became tramps, so that, as a body, they were never heard of more. Of the Irregulars many remained faithful; and, being sent out into the district, rescued a party of beleaguered Christians—Major and Mrs. Ryves and some railway *employés*—all of whom were safely conducted into the fort with the exception of the lady, who unhappily sank under her fatigues.

At this time the city and suburbs were in open rebellion under the Maulvi already mentioned, whose preaching had commended him as a leader to the disaffected population. His head-quarters were at the Khushru Garden, opposite the railway-station, whither he had conveyed the two guns taken from Lieutenant Harward on the night of the outbreak. Having first secured the bridge of boats, Neill organised an expedition against these rebels. On the 13th the suburbs near the fort were cleared; on the 14th the steamer *Jumna* arrived with further reinforcements; on the 17th a party of volunteers, under Mr. H. D. Willock, the joint magistrate, supported by some men of Neill's famous regiment, the Madras Fusiliers, and by two howitzers under Harward, proceeded up the river, and, in co-operation with another party headed by Neill, drove the rebels from the town. The Maulvi and his followers abandoned their guns and fled; Mr. Court, proceeding to the chief police-station, restored his authority over the town and reinstated his officers; on the 18th the "station" (White Town) was occupied, and the cantonments were penetrated.

Unfortunately, the exposure and licence of the past began to tell, in the shape of a violent outbreak of cholera, to which no less than forty of the priceless Fusiliers at once succumbed. Neill immediately thinned the population of the fort by ordering out all non-combatants, and (the re-occupation of the station and cantonment rendering this easier) the epidemic disappeared as suddenly as it had broken out. Drafts of men now arrived daily, and soon nothing remained to hinder the advance upon Cawnpore but the difficulty of procuring transport in a locality that had been so scourged and ravaged. On the 30th, Major Renaud was able to start with a small column. Alas! Wheeler had already capitulated—with consequences that we know.

On the 1st July General Havelock reached Allahabad, and on the 11th joined Renaud at Khága with a strong column of foot and three guns. Next morning they had their first brush with the enemy, headed by Hikmat-Ulla, revolted deputy-collector of Fatehpur. Mr. Willock, being with the "faithful" Irregulars, was put to flight by a charge of the 2nd Bengal Cavalry, no doubt owing to the sympathising of his men, who were soon after disbanded by order of General Havelock. Let it be mentioned, however, that the British officers displayed their usual gallantry, and that the Risáldár (native captain) of the Irregulars was killed bravely doing his duty.

Mr. Willock may now be left, as he has proceeded beyond the limits of his district, and we return to Mr. Court at Allahabad. Here the work of retribution and restoration was in stern progress. Numbers of those who had taken an active part in the disturbances that ensued upon the mutiny of the 6th were in hiding in and about the town, and it was upon them that vengeance was in the first instance directed. On the 22nd July "special commissions" were issued to certain individuals, one of whom was a well-known railway contractor, and the work of reprisal began in fatal earnest. "The result of these measures," writes Mr. Thompson, "was soon visible in a wholesome fear pervading all classes of natives—plundered property was cast into the fields and roads by those who felt that its possession was unsafe." The sentence contains more than, perhaps, was meant. Fear—whether "wholesome" or not, was certainly felt by "all classes"—whether criminal or not. A *terreur blanche* was set up. "Zealously," writes an observer who was present,* "did the commissioners use their powers; and, in the short time which elapsed before their recall, one of these private individuals had sentenced sixty, the second sixty-four, and the civil surgeon fifty-four, to the gallows. No record remains of crime or evidence, but we gather that one man was hanged for having a bag of new copper coin in his possession. . . . . Thirteen were hung another day for a similar offence. Six were hung for plying a ferry for the convenience of the rebels" (by whom they must have been shot if they had refused). Mr. Cust, however, adds that the proceedings of the trained officials, sensible of

* Cust's "District during the Rebellion."—*Calcutta Review.*

responsibility and accustomed to balance proof and disproof, were more deliberate. Indeed, it is to be hoped so.

At all events, Allahabad was now safe. But the country was much disturbed. The usual agrarian outrages set in; landmarks were removed, new proprietors evicted, vendettas enforced, Europeans hunted down. The Prágwál Brahmans spread over the villages, abusing their supposed sanctity and their personal influence to mislead the simple credulous villagers; and the Maulvi flaunted his green banner. When authority recovered the upper hand these tracts were entirely deserted, and great difficulty and delay were experienced before the operations of peace could be renewed there.

It has already been mentioned that the tracts beyond the Jumna had escaped the general demoralisation. Here three chiefs, the Rájás of Mánda, Dáhia, and Barra, had frowned upon all attempts at misconduct, and were prepared to receive the Government officers with open arms and a clear conscience.

Beyond the Ganges, on the other hand, the Rájput clans had seized the opportunity to sweep away all that opposed the resumption of the power that they had forfeited by a long career of idleness and extravagance. Strong in the sympathies of the tenantry, they long continued to maintain a guerilla warfare against the Government that had, in their opinion, caused their losses. They were assisted by escaped convicts and, doubtless, by mutinous sepoys; and it was not till the beginning of 1858 that serious measures could be taken for their suppression. In January a force, under Brigadier Campbell, left Allahabad, which, driving all opposition before it, occupied the Grand Trunk road and surrounding country, as far as Phulpur. Then came fugitive troops from Oude, flying before the column commanded by General Franks,* and causing fresh disorganisation. "Order cannot," concludes Mr. Thompson's *Narrative*, "be said to have been effectually restored until Brigadier Berkeley took the stronghold of Dehion (Daháin) on the 14th of July. With that event the

* Malleson, ii. 328–9.

disturbances consequent on the mutiny may be said to have been subdued in the district of Allahabad." [*Vide* Malleson, iii. 280.]

Some pictures of civil administration in this troublous time have been extracted by Colonel Malleson* from Mr. Cust's most valuable paper. In addition to his other powers, Mr. Court was entrusted with authority for the levying of fines upon offenders, individual and corporate, and for the confiscation of estates. Lord Canning went to Allahabad in the beginning of 1858, and took over the local government from Mr. J. P. Grant, who, having administered firmly during a most trying time, returned to Calcutta to take up the post of President of the Supreme Council. The Lieutenant-Governorship of the province was vacant, and Allahabad became henceforth marked out as the future seat of government.

Supported by the immediate presence of the Governor-General (no longer fettered by any assessors), Mr. Court proceeded with his arduous duties. In all things he displayed the moral and intellectual resources of a well-born and well-trained English officer. His work was varied and complicated to a degree bordering on distraction. Unadjusted items, of the smallest and also of the largest amount, swelled his inefficient balance, arising from payments that had often to be made on the spur of the moment, and must sometimes have been unsupported by vouchers. Thus, it is asserted by Mr. Cust that spies and emissaries had to be occasionally rewarded by being allowed to dip their hands into a bag of silver and appropriate as much as they could grasp! Supplies of cash, and not of cash only, had to be constantly made to advancing columns, and assistance promptly rendered to officers of the commissariat and ordnance departments. The writer calls to mind a case in which one of such items remained unadjusted for nearly ten years. At the same time, though treasure was continually pouring in from Calcutta, revenue had in due course to be realised from the villages, wasted by war and rapine, and from fields often deserted

* Vol. iii. pp. 442 ff.

by their cultivators; or, where not realised, formal proceedings of suspension, equally of course, had to be recorded. For, as Mr. Cust (himself a high revenue authority) most justly remarks, it often became "a grave moral question how far a government is justified in demanding the payment of taxes when it has notoriously failed in its duty of protection." Other features of the district officer's care-ridden career will be found most graphically pictured in Mr. Cust's pleasant paper, among which may be noted the keeping of an unpaid hotel. For his house at Allahabad became known as the rendezvous of visitors; and many survivors, officials and travellers, must still recollect the rough but ready hospitality of "The Red Lion."

"No wonder," concludes Mr. Cust, "if some grey hairs showed in his beard, if his heart sometimes palpitated from over-excitement, and his liver sometimes troubled him. . . . . He had much to bear; and the rebellion fell heavily on his estate, his family, and his health. He was mentioned in no despatches,* the thanks of Government reached him not; and, when he saw that the tide had turned and that the country was saved, he hurried to England, on the chance of rest bringing back tone to his body and change of scene restoring equanimity to his mind."

Mr. Court is, I believe, still enjoying the *otium cum dignitate* of a country gentleman in his native land. If the labours of other officers were more martial and, so far, more conspicuous, few of his contemporaries exceeded him in those equally useful exertions by which the work of the sword is supported and rendered possible.

* *Vide* Extract from Dunlop in introductory remarks.

CHAPTER VII.

BENARES AND AZAMGARH.

THE Benares division, at the time of the outbreak, was of great extent, containing nearly twenty thousand square miles, with a population of some nine millions, of which all but about ten per cent. was of Hindu origin and creed. Taken alphabetically the districts may be thus described :—

1. AZAMGARH, 2,565 square miles, with a population of about one million and a quarter. More than a quarter of the area was barren, consisting either of salt-desert, swamp, or ravine. The district officer was, at first, Mr. Horne, afterwards relieved by Mr. R. H. Davies. This officer subsequently, as Sir Henry Davies, became Lieutenant-Governor of the Panjab. Other civil officers did service of various kinds during the troubles at Azamgarh in the vicinity, but by far the most conspicuous of the non-military leaders were two planters: one, Mr. Venables, ultimately died of wounds received in action, and his deeds were commemorated by Lord Canning *; the other, Mr. M. P. Dunn, long survived the mutiny, but no public recognition of his conduct was ever made, though (as the Commissioner pointed out at the time) "it was he who first persuaded Venables to return; and his courage and daring on every occasion is (*sic*) spoken of by everyone with admiration." †

* *Vide* Despatch (Canning to Chamber of Commerce), Malleson, vol. ii p 546

† Commissioner's *Narrative*, dated 6th November 1858.

2. BENARES. This district is only 996 square miles in area, but the number of inhabitants is—and was even then—large for the area, being three quarters of a million at least. It was therefore an unusually dense population, living in towns, on market gardens, and on highly-cultivated farms. The chief town, or city, stands about half-way between Dehli and Calcutta; the site of an ancient Brahmin settlement, and containing some thousand Hindu temples, in addition to bathing-places and shrines. Besides its sanctity Benares is an important entrepôt, both of manufactures and agricultural produce. The chief civil officers were Messrs. H. C. Tucker, the commissioner; F. B. Gubbins, judge; F. M. Lind, district-officer; and two gentlemen who have since become better known, the late Archibald S. Pollock; and E. G. Jenkinson, at present (1883) the very successful police under-secretary in Ireland. These officers held, as will be presently seen, firm possession of their posts throughout. The English town is at Secrole, some three miles away from Benares.

3. GHÁZIPUR. A district of 2,167 square miles, with a population of about a million and a quarter, is an alluvial plain, permeated by three rivers, the Ghágra, Gumti, and Ganges, the last of which, in the rainy season, is often four miles across from shore to shore. The lands are much exposed to flooding, and the population has long been depressed in character and decreasing in numbers. The magistrate of this district was Mr. Andrew Ross, an officer who is believed to have served in the Royal Navy before entering the service; and among his subordinates were Mr. John Bax—afterwards Bax-Ironside, C.B. —and Mr. Leslie Probyn, brother of the well-known General Sir Dighton Probyn, K.C.S.I. and V.C. As will be seen, the mutiny administration was successful.

4. JAUNPUR, area 1,555 square miles, and population about one million, had long enjoyed the doubtful blessings of a "permanent settlement" of the land-revenue, under which the following state of things had come about—[the quotation is from an official report of the period]:—

The changes in the ownership of land have occurred in all cases at the instance of the civil courts. Old officials, law-agents, and money-lenders, are still supplanting those of the original proprietors that are left. . As a rule they are hard, exacting, bad landlords. . . . . Their large profits are not expended in improving the estates. . . . the tenantry are hostile, abject, and thoroughly discontented.

Mr. H. P. Fane was the chief, or district magistrate at the commencement of the outbreak; but his place was ere long vacated, and Mr. Lind, from Benares, took charge of the district. It need only be here added that the country is generally flat and fertile, and that the chief town is a decayed Musalmán settlement.

5. The last district to be mentioned is the enormous county called, from its chief town, MIRZAPUR. It consists of no less than 5,217 square miles, though the population hardly exceeded a million in those days. The district abounds in forests and mountain ranges (which is a characteristic more favourable to the sportsman and the lover of nature than to the farmer or merchant), though the town of Mirzapur, being on the bank of the Ganges, has some note as a mart for produce, and for manufactures of carpets and piece-goods, and is also an entrepôt for cotton. The district at the time was in charge of Mr. St. George Tucker.

Another enormous tract, originally attached to the Benares division, is Gorakhpur, a fragment of the ancient kingdom of Kosila, or Audh. But it is not included in the Commissioner's narrative, and was not the scene of any considerable events. It is an alluvial and verdant tract lying at the foot of the Nepalese Himalayas. It was abandoned in August 1857, and, after lying vacant for some time, was occupied on behalf of the Government by Sir Jung Bahádur, the minister of the Alpine kingdom, in January 1858. The district was then for some time made into a separate commissionership. The attempts of Messrs. Wynyard, Paterson, and Bird to maintain order, in the teeth of insurmountable difficulties, are well told by Malleson (vol. iii. p. 447 ff.)

It has been said above that the "Station," or White-town, of

Benares is at Secrole; this is a village three miles N.W. of the city, containing the public offices, cantonments, and garden-houses, or "bungalows" of the officers civil and military; also, in 1857, a mint. In May the garrison consisted of the 37th Native Infantry, the 13th Irregular Cavalry, and a portion of a Sikh Regiment of Ludiána, in all about two thousand troops. About the middle of the month arrived news of the mutinies at Meerut and Dehli, and the terrible sufferings that they had drawn on the Europeans at those places. The people of Benares, as it chanced, were at that time suffering from a dearth of food, and were consequently in a somewhat dangerous frame of mind; and the Hindu sepoys, scarcely concealing their fanatical aspirations for a revolution, sent away their guru or chaplain, lest (as they said) he should sustain harm in the coming troubles. Messrs. Gubbins and Lind at once addressed themselves to these present evils, now patrolling the streets with parties of horse, now trying their powers of persuasion to obtain diminution of the prices demanded by the grain-dealers, or listening to the reports of emissaries who—as soon appeared—gave them truer information of the feelings of the native soldiery than was obtained by the military commanders themselves. The Mint was fixed on as the *rendezvous* for the Christians in case of serious alarm; but on further consideration this plan was so far modified that the civil residents were to congregate first at the collector's office, a lofty building adjoining the Treasury. Here were amassed not only the cash belonging to the State, but also the jewels of the Ex-Ráni of the Panjab (the mother of H.H. the Maharaja Dhulip Singh). It was hoped that the civilians, by collecting there in arms, would be enabled to overawe the guard and save all this property, valued at more than a quarter of a million of money.

It is memorable that this plan, which was crowned with eventual success, was not decided on without opposition from high military authority. The officer commanding the artillery (afterwards to acquire great renown as Major, and ultimately

General, Olpherts) concurred with the chief engineer in thinking that the Secrole positions were all untenable, and half succeeded in impressing his strong will upon Colonel Gordon, the officer next in rank to the Brigadier, and inducing him to order a retreat upon the fort of Chunar. But Mr. Lind, strongly dissenting, refused to stir from his post without the decision of a council; and when the council met, and Mr. Tucker, the Commissioner, seemed also inclined to give way, Lind and Gubbins used the strongest arguments against the movement. "I," said the Judge, "will go on my knees to you, to beg that you will not leave Benares." "And I," replied Gordon, "am right glad to hear you say so. The move on Chunar would be a false one, I see, and I was persuaded into approving of it against my will."

This amendment, then, being finally disposed of, the original design (as modified) was carried; and the British officers prepared for the worst. That was on the 3rd of June. Next day the council reassembled to discuss the disarming of the 37th Native Infantry, and, while still sitting, were informed of the mutiny at Azamgarh, to be described hereafter. As they were dispersing after having come to a final agreement, the roar of guns was heard from the parade-ground. Obedient to the preconcerted arrangement, the civilians repaired to the Collector's office, well armed, and took possession of the treasure. On their way they were fired at in crossing a bridge; three of them were driving in a carriage, but Mr. Jenkinson was on horseback, and with impulsive heroism threw himself in front of his companions, so as to intercept the cartridges intended for them. Such unselfishness is not often heard of, but it rests on the testimony of Mr. F. B. Gubbins, one of those in the carriage.

The firing that had been heard was due to the attack made upon the sepoy lines by Colonel Neill, at the head of two hundred of the 1st Madras Fusiliers who had just arrived from Calcutta, supported by Olpherts with his half-battery. The sepoys fought well for a few minutes, and the Sikhs, taken by surprise, joined them. But the resistance was quickly overpowered by rapid discharges of grape; the sepoys were dispersed with a loss of two hundred, the loss on the British side being only two officers and the like number of men.

Next day the civilians proceeded to the Mint, which was hastily fortified; the contents of the Treasury were placed under European guard; and Mr. Pollock, who had gone out into the district on the 3rd, began taking active measures to push on the reinforcements that were arriving by driblets from Calcutta. Communication with Allahabad was maintained by Mr. Jenkinson, who took charge of the road with a party of Native Cavalry under Lieutenant (afterwards Major-General) Palliser; and special legislation speedily bore fruit in "a few instances of crime committed after breakfast and avenged before dinner." Jenkinson next proceeded to raise fresh mounted police, whom he sent, under Mr. Chapman, against some Rajputs from a village in the Jaunpur district, who were cutting off communication with Azamgarh. The force returned on 30th June after having inflicted severe chastisement; but the tenacious Rajputs returned to the attack, and marched within nine miles of Benares, only to be again trounced, after which they gave no further trouble.

Messrs. Gubbins and Lind, however, continued to feel natural anxiety for the very important post in their charge (on which, indeed, depended the due advance of the troops from Calcutta to the Upper Provinces), and in this interest pressed earnestly upon the military authorities the need of some more important and—so to speak—aggressive place of strength at Benares than the improvised defences of the Mint. They freely offered convict-labour; and finally obtained sanction to an estimate from the Government, which was not then in a very thrifty mood. The result was the erection of the fortification, irregular but strong, that, standing on the site of an old Hindu castle, commands the approach at Rájghát, whether by water or by land. We must now turn for a while to Azamgarh.

The outbreak of the sepoys at Benares had been precipitated by events occurring in the vicinity. The troops at Azamgarh consisted of the 17th Native Infantry, a regiment that had been lately brigaded with the 19th Native Infantry at Lucknow, and had contracted much intimacy with men of that regiment. In the latter part of May, some men of the 19th being on a visit in the lines of the 17th, a small but discreditable breach of discipline was committed on parade, which Major Burroughs, the officer in command, did not feel competent to notice, as he dared not inflict due punishment in the circumstances by which he was surrounded. But he fortified the Collector's office with loop-holed walls and sand-bags, and placed a gun in position guarded by those of his men whom he deemed most worthy of confidence. On the 2nd June, Mr. Horne, the district officer, attempted in vain to detain some treasure which had been called in from Benares. On the night of the following day a convoy was actually despatched with no less than seven lakhs of rupees under a guard of cavalry. This seems to have been too much for the sepoys, who immediately sprang to arms, shot their English quartermaster-sergeant, and put the officers—civil and military — to flight. The jail-guard joined, releasing the prisoners, and the men at the Collector's office murdered Lieutenant and Adjutant Hutchinson and seized the gun.* The remainder of the white people, male and female, found a temporary refuge on the fortified roof; and, when the coast was clear, retreated on Gházipur. The mutinous sepoys meanwhile pursued the treasure, which they brought back with them to their lines, whence they ultimately departed to Faizábád in Oude. On the 16th Mr. Dunn returned to Azamgarh, accompanied by Mr. Venables and some mounted constables placed at their disposal by the magistrate of Gházipur, their primary object being to search for and, if possible, rescue any refugees who might be lurking in the villages. In this they were successful, as also in getting rid of some men of the 13th Irregular

* The sepoy who shot the Adjutant was afterwards taken by a detective (to whom he rashly confided the narrative of his exploit), while serving as a pointsman on the East Indian Railway. He was tried before the present writer, and hanged: as fine a man as could be seen.

Cavalry, who seemed at first inclined to dispute their possession of Azamgarh. They remained, and were invested with magisterial power by order of the Commissioner. Along with them also remained Messrs. Legge, Dodsworth, and Niblett. It is to be remarked that from the 2nd to the 16th Mr. Niblett, who was the Collector's head clerk, had been sheltered by a Muhamadan colleague named Ali Baksh, who had during all these days continued to frustrate all attempts at the formation of a rebel administration, organised a native committee of public safety, and even contrived to send daily reports to the Commissioner at Benares. Ali Baksh was rewarded by promotion. I do not know whether he still lives, but his name deserves to be recorded perpetually as that of a true hero and faithful servant of an alien Government whose salt he had eaten.

Indeed, anxious as the writer of these pages naturally is to lose no fitting occasion of commemorating the services of his brother-officers of the Covenanted Civil Service, he cannot forbear to call attention to the singular spectacle presented at this crisis by the district of Azamgarh. Abandoned by all its official guardians and administrators, it was dependent on the courage and vigilance of a few planters and subordinate employés. Venables, though in no degree the superior in moral qualities to Dunn, was the better man of business, and assumed the chief authority. It was no sinecure. On the western side the Rajput clans were in open hostility, strengthened by a fortnight's licence. "The police, helpless with terror, the provisional council unable to rule even the neighbouring villages, had not dared to cope with these audacious plunderers; and Mr. Venables soon found that he must try his power against them in the field, or be forced to save his own life by again abandoning the station." [*Official Narrative.*]* His force was small, consisting of 150 of the 65th Native Infantry, seventy-five mounted constables, and an old gun. The enemy were numerous, and

* This narrative, by Mr. Robert Taylor, is one of the best of the series; and it has been a pleasure to use it.

well-provided with fortified places and with military stores. The first attempts against them met with but poor success, and 500 of them stormed the police-station in broad daylight and released some of their friends who had been captured and confined there. About the 12th of July Mr. Venables, having managed to obtain some more (apparently faithful) sepoys, attacked the Rájputs of the Palwár clan at Koilsa. But the sepoys misconducted themselves, and Venables was forced to fall back on Azamgarh, pursued by the enemy at a respectful distance. By the 18th they had arrived, however, within two miles of the city. At this juncture, fortunately, Messrs. Davies and James Simson, civil officers, came in, bringing with them ten military officers marching to join the Gurkha force sent down from Nipal; twenty-five sabres 12th Irregular Cavalry, and a raw levy from Benares under Captain Catania. The bulk of the 65th men at the same time returned to their head-quarters at Gházipur. With the force that remained the attack was resumed, while Mr. Simson remained at Azamgarh with Catania's men for the protection of the public offices, breast-works having been thrown up across the approaches. Some newly-raised matchlockmen were also posted in various parts of the town. Again was Venables doomed to disappointment; he found the enemy too strongly posted for attack. Presently he had to assume the defensive; the defence became a retreat; but for his gun and some of his horsemen he would scarcely have been able to retire, as he did, without serious loss. During the night the question of retreat on Gházipur was seriously discussed, and the only voices for remaining are said to have been those of James Simson, Lieutenant Havelock, and Venables himself; but in the morning the minds of the defenders of Azamgarh were relieved by finding that the enemy had also had their misgivings, and had melted away.

The fight of the day before had been long, and the loss of the enemy turned out to have been more severe than had been at first supposed. The gun had done fatal service with its frequent discharges of grape; the horsemen, led by Venables and Dunn, had used their sabres well; the Palwárs had retired to their villages with the loss of two hundred and fifty of their best men.

After this matters went on quietly till the 28th July, when news arrived of the mutiny of the 12th Cavalry at Sigaoli; and then it was felt that no confidence could be reposed in the detachment of that regiment at Azamgarh. Next day came news of the mutiny at Dinapore, together with a note from Mr. Tucker, the Commissioner at Benares, authorising evacuation, which was accordingly decided on. It was a dreary march, followed by a long line of carts, in which the townspeople were removing their property. The tide of rapine closed on their departure, and the town was given up to plunder before the troops were well clear of the suburbs. With some difficulties and alarms the column achieved its march to Gházipur; but behind them all was confusion. The faithful native employés having shared the evacuation and retreat, there was no material left for a committee of safety. The police-stations, with two exceptions, were deserted by their occupants; the Palwárs seized the town and levied a pecuniary requisition. It deserves to be mentioned that the native officials of Nagra and Muhamadábád continued to conduct the business of their posts. Their names were Asghar Ali and Muhamad Taki.

On the 20th August the Gurkhas arrived under Colonel Wroughton, followed on the 3rd September by Messrs. Wynyard and Birch, C.S.; and on the 20th September Wynyard and Venables, accompanied by a Gurkha force under Colonel Shamshir Singh and Captain Boileau, fought the brilliant action at Mandori (described by Malleson, vol. ii. p. 317 ff.), in which they killed nearly three hundred of the enemy and took three guns. On this occasion Venables helped to take the first gun, and killed three rebels with his own hand. No wonder if the rebels offered a reward for his head. Mr. Bird soon after took another party of Gurkhas out, who demolished two forts and reoccupied the station of Mahul; and this, for the time, restored the Government throughout the district.

Soon after Mr. Pollock assumed charge, and—while amusing the Palwárs with negotiations—fell upon the Gorakhpur rebels who had been driven towards him by the Gurkhas. Aided by the fire of a gun well-directed by Mr. Hercules Ross, C.S., Mr. Pollock drove them across the river; and then, turning his attention to the Palwárs, set out at the head of a sufficient force, to make a tour through their country. Having made certain examples of them and demolished some of their strong places, he brought them to terms; and although the district was afterwards twice invaded, the Palwárs never gave any further trouble. The remaining operations in the district of Azamgarh were chiefly military; and the successful campaigns of Longden, Lugard, and Lord Mark Kerr have been amply described by the accomplished historian of the mutiny. The town—which had been occupied by the notorious Kunwar Singh—was finally recovered on the 14th April 1858; but the victory was dearly bought by the death of the gallant Venables, who was mortally wounded in the pursuit of the enemy on that occasion. Kunwar Singh was soon after driven out of the district, in which order was promptly and permanently restored.

CHAPTER VIII.

GHÁZIPUR, JAUNPUR, AND MIRZÁPUR.

CONSIDERABLE space has been given to Azamgarh, the events there having been of a peculiar type. The original outbreak there exercised a powerful influence on events in the neighbouring districts, especially Benares; and that most important post itself owed its ultimate safety to the final success of the military leaders in Azamgarh, directed and aided by the fighting planters. We have now to see what had been going on in the remaining districts.

The events in the district of Gházipur may be disposed of briefly. Of the chief, Mr. A. Ross, the Commissioner—Mr. F. Gubbins—observes that, "his prudence and firmness as magistrate had a great effect in preserving the peace of his jurisdiction." From the circumstances mentioned in the opening description this had always been a troublesome district to manage; and minor disturbances soon broke out. Luckily, in spite of the Treasury being full of cash, the troops—the 65th Native Infantry—did not mutiny as was so generally the case elsewhere. But the mutiny at Azamgarh had its effect there, no less than at Benares. The fugitives from Azamgarh arrived, as we have seen, in safety, but the district rose behind them; by the 6th of June civil war became almost universal throughout the Ghazipur district. "The police were helpless, and robberies were perpetrated to the very door of the Court House itself." The treasure was sent into Benares by steamer;

"martial law was proclaimed," implying the subordination of the civil power; and military officers conducted expeditions to the worst-behaved parts of the district where they inflicted exemplary punishment; by the 16th order seemed in a fair way to being restored. On the 7th July, however, Mr. Bax had to take a party (native horsemen and a handful of British troops) for the protection of an indigo factory belonging to a Mr. Matthews, and to destroy a recalcitrant village. On the 14th came news of the outbreak of Kunwar Singh at Arrah, followed on the 27th by the yet more disquieting announcement of the mutiny of the native garrison at Dinapore. The 65th had already announced that their own loyalty was only conterminous with that of their brethren at this station, so that the rising there might be taken as the signal for a rising at Gházipur. "Still they stood in unstable loyalty; why, no one knows." Mr. Bax proceeded with Vincent Eyre to Arrah, and the news of the memorable relief of Arrah was followed up by the disarming of the 65th, which was effected without bloodshed. Mr. Ross had the satisfaction (in which he stood almost alone among his colleagues at the time) of being able to carry on his duties in comparative tranquillity. A part of those duties was, however, of extraordinary character and exceptional usefulness—namely the collection of stores, supplies, and carriage for the European troops constantly hurrying westward. These modest labours deserved, perhaps, more recognition than they have hitherto received.

In 1858 trouble was renewed. Eastern Gházipur became demoralised by the wake of Kunwar Singh's final retreat. "Far from the centre station, unpierced by roads, bounded by two great rivers, by crossing either of which the fugitives would be in another province and under another law, that tract seemed marked out for an Alsatia." The conditions and elements of disturbance that had always characterised it, and under which the police, even in the most tranquil times, had always been unequal to their work, now broke forth in full conflagration.

Fugitive sepoys, whose homes were in its inaccessible hamlets, formed so many centres of petty rebellion; the whole region was a very ant-hill of microscopic confusion. About the middle of May serious measures were taken with it; and Mr. Leslie Probyn, C.S., having obtained the aid of a party of troops under Colonel Cumberlege, took the fortified village of Baragáon, and returned to Gházipur, after destroying the houses of the ring-leaders. South of the Ganges, however, order was not so soon restored; rapine and arson raged without repression; every person who had served the State or aided European individuals was murdered with every circumstance of atrocity. The police were thoroughly cowed by this reign of terror; "no language can describe too strongly the utter disorganisation of the end of June."

Early in July Mr. Bax moved out to Ballia. The rebels had broken down a bridge on his line of advance, but he forded without opposition. Ballia was evacuated; and leaving Mr. Probyn there with a garrison of Sikhs, Mr. Bax marched towards the confluence of the Ghágra and Ganges. Here he was in some danger of being surrounded, but was relieved by the advance of Brigadier Douglas. For a general view of this officer's operations the reader should consult Malleson, vol. ii. p. 484 ff. The story of the civil administration of Gházipur presents no further important features. The subdivision of Zamánia was held throughout August, the north and east were completely tranquillised, by the end of October the entire district was cleared of rebels. Bax was made C.B., the only subordinate officer who (so far as I know) obtained that distinction.

Turning to Jaunpur, we find what Mr. Taylor calls "a strange scene"; of which the opening is easy, though not particularly pleasant, to relate. The conditions mentioned in our preliminary description were sufficient to justify the belief that the district was not likely to escape the contagion of disaffection and disturbance. The estates had largely changed hands; but the ex-proprietors, though ruined, remained on the spot and maintained their local influence. Absorbed in agrarian quarrels the natives of the district seem to have made no preparation for the coming troubles; the Christian planters had been more prescient, and had collected together in the chief town as a place of safety. On the morning of the 5th June, the Europeans being all collected at the Collectorate with arms in their hands, the news of the outbreaks at Benares and Azamgarh arrived. The Treasury-guard (a detachment of the Sikh Regiment that had been so unfortunately implicated at Benares) was roused to fury by the tidings of their comrades' slaughter. They shot their commandant; and meeting Mr. Cuppage, the joint-magistrate galloping down to the jail, they murdered him likewise. Each man then helped himself to a bag of the silver coin in the Treasury, and the whole detachment, with arms in their hands, marched off in good order to Lucknow.

The English first sought safety in the house of Rai Hingan Lal; but being driven thence by a turbulent Rajput clan, they retired upon a factory at some distance in the country, whence they were brought in to Benares on the 9th June by a party of volunteers who went out for the purpose. No sooner had they departed than "the plunder of the Treasury was completed by decrepit old women and street boys, who had never seen a rupee in their lives"; the bungalows of the English were plundered and destroyed. A committee was improvised by the natives, as at Azamgarh; and Mr. Fane, returning for a day, formally installed Raja Sheoghulám, the head of the Dubés (the clan mentioned above) as temporary chief. This latter appointment does not appear to have been popular. The peace of the town was disturbed; in the district at large no vestige of authority remained, anarchy became universal. "Those who had lost their estates under our rule," so writes Mr. Taylor, "thought this a good time to regain them; those who had not, thought they could make a little profit by plundering their weaker neighbours; the bolder spirits thought to secure more brilliant advantages by intercourse with the rebel powers in

Oude; and in this state they remained till the arrival of the Gurkhas on September 8th restored a semblance of authority to the British Government." Charge was then assumed by Messrs. F. M. Lind, and E. G. Jenkinson, C.S., both of whom have been already mentioned in these pages; with them being Mr. Patrick Carnegy, an "uncovenanted deputy" of whom an account may be found in Malleson, vol. ii. p. 339. Of all these officers it is recorded that they performed the work of soldiers in addition to their own; accompanying the Gurkhas throughout the campaign that led to the reoccupation of the district, during which they "exhibited great gallantry in the field, and were most indefatigable in the performance of their duties." (Commissioner to Government, 6th November 1858.) Nor should the names of those persons be forgotten who, though not in the service of the State, came forward in the general trouble to aid in the maintenance of order. Of such were Messrs. Waleski, indigo-planters who, "out of pure loyalty, accompanied the authorities on their return to Jaunpur, and then shared the whole of the subsequent campaign. . . . Hingan Lál, who gave shelter. . . . to the Jaunpur fugitives. . . . Madhu Singh, Zemindar of Bisharatpur, who sheltered a considerable party of planters . . . and has ever since proved a loyal subject of Government . . . Rája Mahesh Narain, ever since the re-occupation a warm partisan of ours, giving us a number of matchlockmen to assist our police, and rendering every other assistance in his power," and Rája Sheoghulám Dubé, mentioned above.* Rai Hingan Lál re-established the outpost of Kirákat, and was appointed Deputy-Magistrate and Collector; the forces of the other outposts were strengthened, and strict orders were issued that the officials in charge should engage in no rash adventures; the southern and eastern tracts began to settle down; a reinforcement was even sent to aid the garrison of Azamgarh; and a rebel leader (Irádat Jahán), who had constituted himself *Naib Názim*, was attacked, and made a stubborn

* Commissioner, *ubi suprà*.

resistance. He collected a force, and held out in his house, which he had fortified. Guns had to be employed, on which he surrendered at discretion ; and, being sentenced by court-martial, was hanged along with another Muslim chief. This was on the 28th September; and the next day witnessed a similar expedition against the fort of another rebel leader, a Hindu named Amr Siṅgh, who had been planning an attack upon Jaunpur. A fight ensued, in which Amr Singh was killed, with some fifty of his men. After some minor operations, the Magistrate, Mr. Lind, returned to Jaunpur with his force on the 5th October. A few days later, he took the field again with the force under Colonel Wroughton, on the tidings that Mehndi Hasan, a *Názim* from Oude, had collected five thousand men at Sultánpur, with whose aid he proposed to attack Jaunpur. On the 19th October the expedition arrived at Singra Mau, and seized the Zemindar, after a good deal of trouble. The force then advanced cautiously through high autumn-crops, and surprised the leaderless foe, who was routed with great slaughter. The rebels evacuated their fort at Chanda, and joined the force under the *Názim*, which, by this time, had reached Hasanpur. Finding that a great number of ex-sepoys were rallying round the hostile standard, Mr. Lind deemed it advisable to hurry up Colonel Longden, for which purpose he left his camp and hastened to Jaunpur. During his absence, however, the Gurkhas attacked the enemy, whom they routed with great loss, capturing his guns, seven in number. This action (fought 20th October) will be found described by Malleson (vol. ii. p. 319 ff). Longden then returned to Jaunpur, from which, however, he again moved on Singra Mau on the 22nd November. Unable to make head against the increased force of the Názim —now swollen to 16,000 men—Longden held a council of war, by whose advice he once more fell back on Jaunpur. The ruffians of the neighbourhood took heart ; the police were driven from their posts ; a loyal native, Pandit Kishn Narain, was beaten at Tigra on the 24th December, and forced to join his superior officers at Jaunpur. No further disaster ensued. The rebels did not pursue their advance; Rája Mahesh Narain watched them with his levies; and "no further occasion for military support occurred till after General Franks's final departure from the district on the 19th February." The Nizám's motley array was finally attacked and dispersed by Sir E. Lugard, who passed into Sháhábád in the beginning of May. The only subsequent event of importance was an attack on the town of Machli-Shahr later on in the same month, but the townspeople defended themselves with resolution till relieved by the civil authorities. And thus ended the troubles in the Jaunpur district, in a manner most creditable to all concerned. Mr. Lind, an officer of remarkable capacity, has since passed away, unrewarded in this world, save by the consciousness of duty well-performed.

While these things were going on in the northern and eastern parts of the Division, it is not to be supposed that the wide tract to the south, between the boundaries of the Benares district and those of the independent State of Rewa, could escape the epidemic. The great extent and wild character of the district of Mirzápur have been already stated. At the time of the outbreak, Mr. St. G. Tucker, the district magistrate, had for his military force a wing of a Sikh corps, with which he took post at his cutcherry on the 21st May on hearing the sound of firing to the eastward. It was soon ascertained that the discharges were but a part of the noisy celebration of a native wedding; on which discovery the officers returned to their dwellings, leaving the Sikhs encamped at the office. On the 7th arrived a portion of the 47th Native Infantry, under Colonel Pott; but by this time the Bengal sepoys had become anything but popular with the British, and the gallant Colonel was persuaded to grant furlough to all but a few trusted men. On the 8th, the Sikhs were called in from Allahabad, and departed with some treasure in their charge, leaving a quantity of arms and ammunition in the magazine. Colonel Pott at once threw into the river the spare cartridges and the nipples of the muskets, thus reducing that element of danger to a minimum; the rest of the treasure was at the same time taken to Benares by a river-steamer. On the 9th the British denizens of Mirzápur became alarmed by sinister rumours, and fled to the neighbouring fortress of Chunár, leaving Mr. St. G. Tucker to bear the brunt alone. On the 10th he availed himself of the arrival of an exceptional body of sepoys (belonging to the 50th Native Infantry, who had brought in a prisoner from Nagode) to march out a few miles and chastise some marauders who had plundered the property of the East India Railway Company. On the 13th a party of the 1st Madras Fusiliers (Neill's Regiment) arrived, and accompanied a detachment of the 47th in a punitive expedition against an offending village on the right bank of the Ganges, near the border of the Allahabad district. The inhabitants of this village (called Gaura) had been peculiarly daring in their misconduct, and prepared for resistance; but the men of the 47th were well handled, and while the white soldiers attacked the rebels in front, crossed the river with the view of taking them in the rear. Some of the leaders were captured, but the surrounding had been incomplete, and the bulk of the rebels made their escape. The right bank of the river was pacified by this step, and by an almost simultaneous movement under Mr. P. Walker, an "uncovenanted" deputy magistrate; but the left bank required more serious exertions. Here a number of townships that had fallen into the possession of the Rája of Benares were still the homes of the dispossessed Rájput clan, to whom they had originally belonged; and their chief proclaimed himself Rája of the Hundred of Bhadüi, and appointed two agents for the collection of the revenue. Not content with this display of independence, he then enrolled a force, with the aid of which he plundered his weaker neighbours, and closed the Grand Trunk Road leading from Calcutta to the North-West. The management of the Rája of Benares's estates was at that time in charge of

Mr. Moore, C.S., the Joint-Magistrate of Mirzápur; and this officer offended the people by doing his duty and vindicating the rights of the Rája. A native agent contrived to obtain possession of the persons of the rebel chief and one of *his* agents; and the pair, being tried and condemned by a court-martial, were promptly hanged. Sentence of death was at once passed in return upon Moore by the popular *Vehm;* and measures were taken to carry it into effect. On the 4th July this officer arrived at the Indigo Factory of Páli, bringing with him another set of brigands whom he had taken captive. The house was presently surrounded by the followers of the late chief of Bhadui; and Moore and the two managers of the factory, being captured in a sortie, were forthwith put to the sword. Moore's head was cut off and carried to the chief's widow, who had offered three hundred rupees for it; Lieut. Woodhouse and a party of H. M. 64th, who came too late for rescue, had only the moderate satisfaction of burying the bodies. Next day they were joined by Mr. Tucker with some of the 47th Native Infantry, and a planter named Chapman came up from another direction. All was in vain, the murderers could not be surrounded; and they escaped, for the time at least. Their flight, however, accelerated the pacification of the district, which was not again disturbed for more than a month. But on the 11th August disturbance was renewed by the irruption of the Dinapore mutineers escaping from their defeat at Arrah by Vincent Eyre. They remained in the neighbourhood, subsisting by plunder, till the 20th, when they set their faces in the direction of Mirzapur, some fifteen hundred strong. About seventeen miles from the town, they were encountered by three hundred men of Her Majesty's 5th (now the Northumberland) Fusiliers, and were ingloriously routed at the first fire. They fled into the Allahabad district. On the 14th of the same month another part of the district was invaded by a party of mutineers from Hazáribágh, and on the 8th September the redoubted Kunwar Singh also visited its confines. Both parties, however, passed through into independent principalities without doing much damage. Charge of the southern part of the district was then made over to Mr. Mayne, the energetic officer already mentioned in connection with the Banda district, and his exertions were successful in maintaining safe transit on the Grand Trunk Road. October went by tranquilly; an "unpassed" young officer, named Elliott, conducted a successful attack to the north-west, in which, with some Sikhs and the Benares police-levy, he chastised the people of two notorious villages there; the guns and stores that had been collected at Mirzápur were consigned to the fortress of Chunár. Rebel bands traversed the district; but the popular mind had now righted, and they met with no sympathy. On the 16th December some policemen were murdered on the Rewa border by some villagers who escaped. The magistrate then proceeded to attack the Chandels of Bijaigarh, who had broken out in furtherance of a family feud. A claimant to the chiefship had proclaimed himself "Rájah"; and had driven away the Tahsildár (native sub-collector) who had attempted to serve him with a summons to appear and answer for his presumption at Mirzápur. On Mr. Tucker's approach, the pretender fled into the forest, where he was attacked on the morning of the 9th January 1858, after a long night-march. Several of the rebels were killed on the spot, others were taken and brought to justice, a quantity of stolen property was recovered, and the residue of the offenders fled across the river Sone. Soon after this it became apparent to Mr. Tucker that the Rájah of Singraoli was giving them countenance, and preparing to defend the fort of Gahrwár, in which some of them were probably harboured; and a messenger was sent to warn him of the probable consequences. But the proclamation of the amnesty stayed further proceedings; and thus the story of Mirzápur in revolt comes to an abrupt termination. Besides Mr. St. G. Tucker and his assistants Elliott and Walker, the Commissioner's report makes favourable mention of the Rája of Kantit and his brother.

CHAPTER IX.

ROHILCUND.

THE province of Rohelkhand, or Rohilcund, as more commonly spelt, was (in the North-Western Provinces) the one in which British power was most completely overthrown. It will not, therefore, present materials for the treatment hitherto pursued. Instead of the narratives of administration more or less maintained, and expedients, often successful, to cope with the disorganisation consequent on the evil deeds of the sepoys and the temporary paralysis of lawful authority, we have now to deal with reports of disaster unretrieved, murder unavenged, attempts at flight, hiding, escape, or—at most—successful adventure.

This sub-province—bounded on the west and south by the Ganges, on the north by the sub-Himalayan range, on the east by Oude—constituted a civil division containing six districts, besides the protected state of Rámpur; it comprised over eleven thousand square miles, and the population was over five millions, of whom the majority were Hindus, a considerable minority being Muhamadans, mostly Pathans descended from Afghan military colonists. The past history of the country is peculiar, and has been more prominently brought before the general reader than that of most parts of India. In the decay of the great Mughul empire of the middle ages it was occupied by Afghan military adventurers, who subdued, without exterminating, the Hindu population, and established a semi-independent principality under a dynasty of their own. In the last half of the eighteenth century, this family being represented by a minor, power devolved upon his guardian, Rahmat Khán—known by his title of "Háfiz," or Protector. The land, being fertile and lying on the borders of Audh (or Oude), attracted the attention of its neighbours. In 1773, when the Mahrattas had been for the time expelled from Hindustan, the Nawáb of Oude, who was titular Vazir of the empire, obtained from the Court of Dehli sanction to chastise the Rohillas, who had been intriguing with the Mahrattas, and to occupy the country. The English ruler, Warren Hastings, agreed to assist, a proceeding for which he was severely censured; his conduct formed part of the Parliamentary impeachment of which Mr. Hastings was afterwards the object, but the count was not sustained. In another work* I have attempted to show that the verdict was a just one, in spite of the unfavourable opinion so strongly expressed by Macaulay in his famous *Essay*. Be that as it may, the resistance of the Rohillas was overcome at the battle of Kattra † (23rd April 1774), where the Protector was slain. After the conquest under Lake, Rohilcund fell, with the rest of Hindustan, into the hands of the British, and became part of what are now called the North-West Provinces.

In 1857 Rohilcund was (as it is still, indeed) a Division, or Commissionership, consisting of six districts, which were called, respectively, Philibhit, Morádábád, Bijnaur, Bareli (or Bareilly), Badaon, and Shahjahanpur. [There was a small *enclave* of independent territory held by the Nuwáb of Rámpur, a descendant of the old reigning family of Rohillas.] The first was a forest tract at the foot of the Kamaon hills, and the events there call for no particular remark. Bijnaur was held for a time, and then perforce abandoned, by the magistrate of the district, Mr. A. Shakespear (*vide* Malleson, vol. iii. p. 400 ff., for an interesting

* *Fall of the Mughul Empire*, 111 ff.

† Or, Miranpur Kattra, the scene of another action in 1857, where his grandson was defeated.

account of the interregnum that ensued). Badaon also ejected its British chief, Mr. William Edwards, whose escape has been glanced at in treating of events at Farrukhábád. Of the doings of the civil officers at the other three we have pretty full accounts, of which an epitome may be here given.

In the district of Morádábád the senior officer was the judge, Mr. (afterwards Sir) John Cracroft Wilson, of whose energetic character a description was given in the chapter on events in Meerut. The other officers were Mr. C. B. Saunders (subsequently Resident at Haidarábád), district magistrate, and Mr. J. S. Campbell (brother of Sir G. Campbell, M.P., and afterwards Judge of the Chief Court of the Punjab). As these officers were not only of much lower standing in the service, but also devoid of his peculiar local knowledge and experience, the Judge volunteered the direction of affairs, an offer which was at once accepted by the Government of Agra. His first step was to ride over to Rámpur and endeavour to enlist the sympathies of the chiefs of that small state on the British side. This was on the 14th of May. On the 18th, hearing that a party of mutineers was approaching from the westward, Wilson went out to attack them with some troopers, who had come to their homes in the district on furlough, and a detachment of the 29th Native Infantry, of which the head-quarters were stationed at Morádábád. The troopers behaved well, and a number of prisoners were taken, with cash in their possession, who turned out to belong to the 20th Native Infantry, a detachment that had mutinied—as already related—at Muzafarnagar. Next morning, the force having gone back to Morádábád, some more mutineers were seized in that station, and one of them was shot by a man of the 29th. Unhappily, the dead man proved to be brother to another of the 29th, and on this becoming known some men of that corps—who had doubtless been already tampered with and prepared for mutiny—hurried to the jail where the prisoners were confined. With the connivance of the guard they threw open the jail, releasing all the convicts, of whatever class. Wilson mounted his horse and went to the spot, accompanied by some military officers; but, finding the task beyond the strength of his party, turned round and galloped off to a neighbouring garden where there was a body of the Nuwáb's cavalry encamped. Here he was refused assistance in insolent terms; but, not to be baulked, he next hastened to the lines of the 29th, where he found that the adjutant of the regiment had already gone after the convicts with a party of faithful sepoys. Having persuaded a non-commissioned officer to follow him with a few men, Wilson pursued and captured some of the convicts, having been in the pursuit at one moment surrounded and obliged to shoot three of them in self-defence. Some villagers came to the spot on hearing the firing, and with their aid nine more were secured. Altogether, including captures made by the adjutant, the officers had recaptured no less than 150 of the escaped prisoners. That day the ladies took refuge in the Court-house and in another building, where they were resolutely guarded by some natives, the head of the Collector's office (Jawád Ali) standing sentry over the door with a drawn sword. In the afternoon the Rámpur cavalry were reported by their native commandant to be in a state of insubordination amounting to mutiny; and a parade of the Company's troops in undress was ordered for 5 P.M. At that hour the Judge proceeded, purposing to address the men, and rode up to the guns which were pointed at him, the artillerymen standing by them with lighted portfires. Overawed by his bold bearing, they let him pass without firing. The British officers joined him here; but the sepoys had not paraded as ordered. Being allowed to provide themselves with ball-cartridge, however, and assured that no treachery was meant, they at length emerged from their huts, and assembled on the parade-ground. A hollow square having been formed, Mr. Wilson delivered his harangue, concluding by swearing upon the Bible that he would use his influence with the Governor-General to pardon the past offences. The men took an oath of fidelity in turn; confidence was restored; and a general feeling ensued that all was safe for the time. Next day the native officers busied themselves in soothing the men, a party of whom followed Lieutenant Clifford and a party of troopers in punishing some Gujars of a village eight miles off, who had opened prematurely the campaign of plunder.

On the 21st a mob from Rámpur advanced on Morádábád flying the green flag of martyrdom, and led by a policeman of that city dressed in green, in token of being a soldier of the Crescent. Wilson went out to meet them at the bridge of boats, accompanied by some troopers and a party of the 29th, under Captain Faddy, of that regiment. The leader and a dozen others were arrested, and the rest fled; the prisoners were handed over to the Rámpur authorities on the following day. The next ten days were signalised by minor adventures and expeditions, in some of which the 29th men showed a good spirit, and not a day passed without the untiring Judge going to their lines and conversing with the native officers and men.

But the fact was that all these exertions were in vain. With the exception, possibly, of Sikh and Gurkha corps, every regiment in the Bengal army had long since been inoculated with the virus; and on the 1st of June rumours became current that the brigade at Bareilly had mutinied *en masse*. It soon became certain that the 29th would follow the example, and the civil officers attempted to remove the treasure. While loading it on tumbrils they were guarded with wonderful fidelity by two native officers, who at length interposed their own bodies between the Judge and the Collector on one side and the loaded muskets levelled at them on the other. The officers, civil and military, then thought, and thought rightly, that they had done all in their power. A little after 3 o'clock, in a blazing sun, four English officers, four ladies, and a discharged British gunner, set off on their forlorn march to Meerut, attended by twenty-five troopers of the 8th Irregular Cavalry and some of the furlough men. On the road they met with much kindness. "Tears were shed, and milk was offered by villagers while we waited at their village" for the officers of the 29th, who never appeared. On the bridge at Garhmukteswar the refugees were met by Mr. Fleetwood Williams; and about 5 o'clock in the morning of Friday, June 5th, they reached Meerut. Here the British refugees were hospitably received by their companions in misfortune, while the faithful horsemen of their escort were promoted on the spot by the general commanding the division.

Thus ends the narrative of the mutiny at Morádábád, and of the attempts made by civil officers to check or retard it. For some time to come Mr. Wilson and his troopers were occupied in collecting revenue and keeping the peace on the eastern side of the Meerut district, separated from Rohilcund by the river Ganges, as already related in our chapter dealing with events in that district. It was not till towards the end of October that he was again engaged in the affairs of Rohilcund.

In the meantime, we may turn to see what had been going on at Bareilly, the chief town of the division. Here were posted Messrs. Robert Alexander, the Commissioner (an accomplished gentleman of good Irish family), G. D. Raikes and D. Robertson, Judges; J. Guthrie, district magistrate; G. B. Pasley, joint magistrate—all of the Civil Service; Drs. Hay (civil surgeon) and Hansborough (superintendent of jail), with Dr. Buch (Principal of college), and several minor officials. The force (consisting of half a battery of field artillery, the 8th Irregular Cavalry, the 18th and 68th Regiments Bengal Native Infantry), formed a brigade commanded by Brigadier Sibbald, C.B. There were also a number of clerks and European tradesmen. The ladies and children were sent to Naini Tál, in the Kamaon hills, on the receipt of news of the Meerut mutiny and massacre; on the 31st May the infantry and artillery broke loose from the control of their officers, but the cavalry were still considered staunch. Indeed, in the earlier days of the Mutiny, it was universally hoped that the "Irregulars" would escape the contagion. And this particular corps had borne privation and done good service in the Burmese war, four years earlier. It will be seen that those who remained true vindicated these expectations by the most faithful and valiant conduct. Mr. Alexander had done what he could to keep the people of the city quiet, but a number of the Muslim citizens were evidently in an excited and untrustworthy condition; the landlord of a township called Kiára, in the immediate vicinity, combined with them, though a Hindu. A grandson of the ill-starred "Protector," of the last century—Khán Bahádur Khán—professed to second the Commissioner's exertions; and a Maulvi attached to the College delivered a discourse at the Mosque, showing that it was unlawful to rebel against the Government. But on the 30th May Khán Bahádur had an interview with Mr. Alexander, in which he candidly declared that "the case was hopeless"; and, taking his hand, said, "Provide for your own safety." When, therefore, on the morrow, the news of the mutiny was known, it found Mr. Alexander to some extent prepared. Though ailing at the time, he contrived to mount his horse and ride to a preconcerted rendezvous, in the cavalry lines; and there he met Colonel Colin Troup, who, in the absence of the Brigadier, proposed that all present should ride with him across country in the direction of Naini Tál. Mr. Guthrie, the magistrate, however, preferred to remain with Lieutenant Mackenzie, of the 8th, and try the effect of one charge with the cavalry. The attempt failed, and then they followed the rest of the fugitives, accompanied by twenty-five good and faithful horsemen, almost all native officers. They did not loiter long on the road, reaching Naini Tál on the morning of the 1st, say seventy-five miles in about twenty-four hours. The station, civil and military, was at once given up to rapine, arson, and murder. Messrs. Robertson, Hay, and R. Orr (the last an uncovenanted deputy-collector), took refuge in the house of a Muhamadan sub-judge, where they were murdered by ruffians of the town. A like fate overtook Messrs. Raikes and Buch. Dr. Hansborough defended his jail till it was broken; he managed to conceal himself during the night, but was taken in the morning and brought before Khán Bahádur, by whose sentence he was put to death. This forms an indelible stain on Khán Bahádur's career. The officers of the 18th Native Infantry were spared by their men, but some afterwards fell slaughtered in a village; others were protected and eventually rescued. The Brigadier was shot by his orderly as he was riding to the cavalry lines. Lieutenant Tucker, of the 68th, was slaughtered by his own men as he was mounting his horse in front of the officers' mess-house. An Irish lunatic, named Healy, appears to have been the only white man who was spared; he was discovered in confinement when Bareilly was re-occupied by Sir Colin Campbell a year later. Altogether, some thirty-five adults were slain in cold blood, besides an almost equal number of children. It is no imputation upon Messrs. Alexander and Guthrie to say that all this crime and suffering might have been diminished, if not entirely avoided, had the place been in charge of a Wilson or a Gubbins. Such men are exceptional; Mr. Alexander, though in bad health and deceived by his native advisers, took all ordinary measures; but the non-official community omitted to send away their families while it was yet possible, or to repair to the appointed rendezvous themselves in good time, and the military officers fell, as soldiers should, in the discharge of their duty. Still, it can hardly be said that all *possible* precautions were taken; and the events at Bareilly are not among the most creditable occurrences of the time. The fact is that the events of the time were so startling that no one who was an eye-witness would think of judging severely officers who, in a position of responsibility, were taken by surprise or thrown off their balance. They were not bred to war—cradled, indeed, in a long and profound peace; used to the most complete and obsequious deference from all by whom they were surrounded; suddenly assailed by forces on which they had never reckoned, and which they were wholly without the means of appreciating or resisting.

The departure of the authorities from Bareilly was clearly unavoidable in the circumstances; they were not blamed; and Mr. Alexander ultimately obtained the 3rd class Order of the Bath.

Khán Bahádur assumed the reins of power, a native officer named Bakht Khán becoming commander of the troops. Many Hindus of distinction joined them at first, the remainder bowed to the blast. The district fell into total anarchy; the people (as Mr. J. Inglis, the writer of the principal *Narrative* relates), "at once rose, not so much in rebellion against the British as against all government; every man" (it is the old story) "prepared to wreak his vengeance on his private foe, or take violent possession of land to which he considered himself to have a claim." A Hindu, named Sobha Rám, who had served in the British Commissariat, was appointed *Diwán* (finance commissioner) of the district; other officials, Hindu and Musalmán, were appointed to various posts; the bankers suspected of pro-British sympathies were tortured and despoiled of their money; on the 11th June the sepoys left for Dehli, under Bakht Khán; an income-tax and property-tax of 10 per cent. was imposed; a semblance of authority was established, which, however, did not extend far beyond the confines of the town. Measures were taken to secure the co-operation of the *Thákurs* (leaders of the Rájput clans), and several of them tendered their allegiance with the usual propitiatory gifts. The British, under Colonel Ramsay, continued to hold the Kamaon hills and to defend Naini Tál against all comers.

CHAPTER X.

ROHILCUND.

Let us now turn to the adjoining district of Sháhjahánpur, where equally tragic events, if on a smaller scale, had been going forward. On the 17th May Mr. Bramly—whom we have seen doing good service in connection with Aligarh—made over charge of the district to Mr. Mordaunt Ricketts, a fatal, if unavoidable, instance of "swopping horses while crossing a stream." Mr. Ricketts was a man of chivalrous courage and romantic character; but he had no local knowledge or influence, and could only adopt the ordinary precautionary measures. The 28th Native Infantry was the corps present, and the officers believed that about five hundred of the men, of whom 150 were Sikhs, might be trusted to remain faithful if the remainder were to rebel. On the 31st May—the day of the Bareilly mutiny, and the date believed to have been fixed on by the conspirators for the general insurrection, had not events been precipitated at Meerut—the regiment broke out. The English were at church, the day being Sunday. A small party of the worst characters among the sepoys went to the building, and rushed in, armed with swords and clubs. Ricketts was at once cut down, the ladies climbed into the belfry. Some other officers were shot in escaping, or near the lines. But the residue were rescued, for the time, by the better-disposed sepoys, and held a council as to their best future course. As the bungalows of the station were by this time in a blaze, it was decided by the next senior officer, Mr. Charles Jenkins, that the non-combatants should be at once escorted to Powain, the fort of a neighbouring native nobleman, who, however, refused (from mere timidity) to take them in. This was the same chief who, in a later stage of affairs, assumed courage to kill the celebrated "Maulvi" of Oude. They accordingly passed on to the civil station of Muhamdi, not far off, where they were hospitably received by the district-officer, Mr. Thomason. Twelve officers, a sergeant, seven ladies, and two children, reached Muhamdi on the morning of the 2nd June. All, I believe, were ultimately slaughtered. Mr. A. Smith, the Assistant-Magistrate, was left behind sick, and was at once murdered by the mutineers. They then proceeded to Rosa, the sugar-factory of Messrs. Carew, which they plundered and burned. The gentlemen in charge of the property escaped with their lives, but afterwards perished in the Oude jungles. Seven Europeans in all had been murdered in the first outbreak; some well-disposed Muslims gave the bodies decent sepulture in the church-yard. The *déchéance* of the British Government was proclaimed, and the usual efforts were made to create a native administration, under a local chief, the Nawáb Ghulám Kádir Khán. The remainder of the official *Narrative* is devoted to a description of this interregnum, and to the characterisation of the numerous faithful natives (official and non-official) who continued to correspond with the Commissioner at Naini Tál; it is observable that of all these only one took service, even ostensibly, under the rebels. Their administration lasted until the 30th April 1858; adopting—so far as possible—the methods, and even the phraseology, of the British system, which was restored without difficulty after the rebels had been driven out. This restoration took place on the 2nd of May.

Meanwhile, affairs in Bareilly had gone from bad to worse. The Hindu leaders chafed under the rule of the Patháns (so are the Indian Afgháns named), and Khán Bahádur found himself obliged to raise a considerable army, which ultimately rose to twenty-nine battalions and forty-four squadrons. These quarrels, and the continued reports of British successes in the surrounding districts, caused constant trouble at Bareilly and elsewhere in Rohilcund; while the unmolested presence and occasional resistance of a large party of British at Naini Tál, under the Commissioner, Colonel (now Lieutenant-General the Hon. Sir) H. Ramsay, acted as a perpetual menace and thorn-in-the-side. On the morning of the 2nd October it was determined to make a display, and an attempt to recover lost prestige. Under pretence of having received a patent with a dress of honour from the rebel Court at Dehli, Khán Bahádur held a solemn durbar. But it was a festival of Herod. Attended by his ministers, in gala costume, mounted on elephants, and followed by a shouting rabble, the usurper proceeded, gorgeously appareled, to a garden near the town, where preparations had been made for the solemnity. He took his seat, facing the crowd, like an Imperial Satrap. After his investiture a royal salute was fired. And then a messenger from Dehli, stepping softly behind the great man, whispered in his ear that the rebel head-quarters there had been stormed by the British, and that the king—his fountain of honour—was a captive in their hands. Turning as pale as his complexion would permit, Khán Bahádur rose and left the assembly; nor did he ever after take part in public civil proceedings.

About this time authentic intelligence began to reach Wilson, on the further side of the Ganges, of the presence of Christian refugees of various classes and of both sexes in the villages of Rohilcund. In the beginning of October, he and his faithful followers (of the 8th Irregular Cavalry) had allowed themselves a fortnight to rest. On the morning of the 20th, being at Aligarh with Mr. Bramly, he opened a letter brought over by a couple of native messengers, addressed to the Chief Civil Officer at Meerut. It proved to be from Captain J. Y. Gowan, and contained "a touching appeal for the rescue of himself and thirty other Christians, survivors of the Bareilly massacre," and now concealed at a village near to the town of Kattra (the scene of Háfiz Rahmat Khán's defeat and death in the last century). Sending word to the Chief Commissioner at Agra, Mr. Wilson left a note for Gowan (written in the Greek character) with Mr. Bramly, which the latter promised to send on to Gowan with the Chief Commissioner's reply, when it arrived from Agra. The purpose of Wilson's note was to inform Gowan that, whatever might be the decision of the Government, he (Wilson) would surely be at a certain ford on the 28th, prepared to rescue the refugees. When the Chief Commissioner's answer arrived, one of the messengers took it, with Wilson's enclosed, to the village where Gowan and some six of his companions, adults and infants, were awaiting his return—with what anxiety may be partly imagined. When the envelope was hastily opened, nothing at first appeared but a precept from the Government offering a reward of ten thousand rupees "to any native who would escort in safety to Aligarh all the Christian refugees now lying concealed in Rohilcund." This was cold comfort; and Gowan, with sinking heart, was in the act of destroying the envelope when he felt the enclosure and read Wilson's Greek note. Great as had been his disappointment was the consequent reaction. It is on record that the seven forlorn creatures, who felt that they had passed from death into life, fell simultaneously upon their knees in the shed where they were lurking, and offered their tribute of pious thanks to the Almighty; and a historical painter could hardly desire a more pathetic subject for his art. Hastening, then, to his earthly protectors, the native villagers, Gowan consulted with them; and the result of the consultation was the despatch of a second letter, written in Greek like that to which it was a reply, and fixing another *rendezvous* for the 29th—the earliest date, as it would seem, on which he could come down with his company to the river-side. Wilson received this note at 7 P.M. of the 28th. In another hour he had started with 100 horsemen and four fast elephants; and the native officer, Buland Khán, was the only person to whom the secret of their destination was confided. It was a service of danger; Khán Bahádur had some five thousand men in the neighbourhood (some of whom soon afterwards fought only too well!), but Wilson secured the boats at the ford of Kuchla (the first that he had named to Gowan), amused the enemy with feints, and then, marching in the cold autumn night thirty miles down the river, reached the place where he expected the refugees, only to meet with fresh disappointment. To cut a long story short, Wilson reached the fort of Kádirganj early on the morning of the 31st, got a breakfast out of the "Nawáb" (as the man in charge called himself), by a mixture of boldness and conciliation, and had the pleasure soon after of receiving a cart, escorted by matchlockmen, and containing Gowan, with Sergeant and Mrs. Belcham, and their children. The good native officer, Buland Khán, when he saw the children, turned aside to hide his tears, and muttered, "And these are the darlings whom those infidels seek to murder—God's curse on them!" On the 2nd November Wilson's party marched with them into Aligarh, and the following morning brought them safely into Meerut. This is only one specimen of the wisdom and courage of this truly remarkable man, whose humanity was only equalled by his energy. First and last, Mr. Wilson was instrumental in rescuing sixty-four Christian refugees in Rohilcund; and surely, of all the gallant "Cucherry Hussars" of the time, none better deserved the honours that he received, or the subsequent prosperity that awaited him in his long retirement in New Zealand. The behaviour of his followers was excellent; and he lived for months among them, speaking Persian and Hindustani, and wearing the dress and accoutrements of a native officer. He told a tale of his meeting Mr. Cocks in this disguise, which showed a vein of humour. On another occasion he rode up just in time to prevent his men being attacked by the daring Paterson Saunders, who mistook them for mutineers. Gowan also did good work through the winter campaign. It was not till May that Wilson returned to Morádábád, which he had left as a fugitive nearly twelve months before; when he did return he was accompanied by Captain Gowan, and by Sergeant Belcham, promoted to Sergeant-Major. Khán Bahádur and his *Diwán* made good their escape, and—so far as I am aware—were never again authentically heard of.

It only remains to state briefly what was the state of popular feeling in Rohilcund at the time. It is Mr. Alexander's deliberate opinion that, neither from fact, document, or oral testimony, can it be inferred that there had been, out of the lines of the regiments, any organised conspiracy for the overthrow of the existing Government, or the establishment of one to take its place. The nature of the administration that ensued aids—in his opinion—to disprove the idea of any pre-existing plot; though there might be deemed to be something suspicious about the early adhesion of the Hindu landholders. But it is quite certain that many Hindus—especially among the moneyed interest—held aloof from the first, and of the rest a good number soon fell away. No early communication with Dehli was traced, as would have been surely the case if the rising, as a political movement, had been pre-concerted; though after Khán Bahádur's usurpation had been consummated, he naturally aspired to the sanction of "Imperial" patronage and countenance.

Furthermore, both among Muslims and Hindus, there were not wanting many who preserved their fidelity under the most searching trials. Thus, Badr-ud-Din, the *Kotwál*, or Head Inspector of Bareilly, Amir Ali, and Zakaria Khán, of the Revenue Department, Abdullah Khán, Kotwál of Philibhit, and a few native subordinates, accompanied their European officers to Naini Tál, and remained there with them, at considerable personal inconvenience to themselves, till the restoration of order in May 1858. Four other native officials remained in their districts, doing such service as was possible; like the former group they were all Muslims. Among non-official natives who either actively assisted the Government, or at least did not assist the rebels, the Commissioner mentions seven prominent Hindus and a Muhamadan. Of the first three (Rajput landholders of Bijnaur district) he says that they "displayed valiant deeds against the common enemy"; adding that "all their strength, and all their pecuniary resources, were put forth to aid the Government and re-establish order"; when unsuccessful, two of them retired beyond the Ganges, the third falling into the hands of the rebels.

Others, it should be added, kept up a correspondence with the Commissioner at Naini Tál; and, though they may have been somewhat in the position of trimmers, it must be remembered that the mere act of writing to the British authorities at such a time was one of considerable danger, and if discovered would have cost them their lives.

CHAPTER XI.

CONCLUSION.

And this brings me to the conclusion of my task. I have not thought it necessary to trace the doings of the civil officers beyond the confines of Hindustán Proper—or the North-West Provinces—of which alone I have personal knowledge, and in regard to which there are full civil official *Narratives* forthcoming. But I hope the reader will pardon me if—seeing that it was here that the revolt arose, and had its focus—I add a few words as to the probable origin of this great disaster. Frequent allusions have been made in the course of our narrative to discontents arising from the transfer of landed property under decrees of Court. But this painful consequence of civilisation would never by itself cause a general rebellion; so long, at least, as the Government was strong. We have seen Mr. Alexander's opinion as to the absence of evidence in respect of a general, pre-arranged, national rising; and we have, I think, had reason, in studying the other narratives, to concur in his view. Had there been such a wide-spread and well-organised plot, it would seem that one of two things must have occurred. Either those loyal tribes, and chiefs, who afterwards held aloof from the revolt or actively joined in its suppression, would have given information to the authorities when they were tampered with or else (if we are to suppose that they were left out) the conspirators and their emissaries must have acted with superhuman wisdom and vigilance in selecting those on whom they practised, and in keeping back all knowledge of what was going on from those they could not bring themselves to trust. On the other hand, general as was the indiscipline and high the prætorian spirit among the native soldiers, the support that they immediately received at places like Dehli and Cawnpore leads me (in my individual capacity) to believe that political discontent, and even political incendiarism, must have had a considerable share in causing the outbreak. I do not say that I am supported by conclusive authority; but it is my own humble though unhesitating opinion that Azimulla, the Nána's Secretary, returned from Europe in 1856 with a readiness to rebel, founded on a belief in the weakness of Britain, and the will and desire of Russia to use the Persian trouble as a stepping-stone to an attack on British India. That he fell into communication with Queen Zinat of Dehli, of whose discontents I had some personal knowledge when serving under Mr. Simon Fraser in the Dehli territory in 1854. That the scheme of restoring the Mughal Empire with Mahratta agency (the *status quo ante* preceding British conquest) about this time occurred to the Queen and to others. And that they saw, in the disorderly and contumacious spirit that had long been growing in the Bengal army, a stock of explosive matter. Lastly, that they found, in the greased cartridges, the spark of fire wherewith to ignite the mine that, as they hoped, was to blow into the air all that obstructed the execution of their designs.

It was certainly, to change the metaphor, a most unhappy coincidence that, while the germs of political discontent were thus fermenting at Dehli, stimulated by events in the Crimea and in Persia, there should have been such a nidus for the reception of the poison as was presented by the condition of the Bengal army. It was at one time thought that religious fanaticism contributed another unhappy factor to the general confusion; and of this there may be some evidence, but it is neither abundant nor strong. That there was anything like a universal fear of Christianity being propagated by force may be fairly doubted. The missionaries were not just then making unusual efforts, nor was the Government giving them any unusual countenance or aid. Their schools, in which the study of the Bible was imperative, were attended as willingly as were the Governmental schools from which the Bible was excluded. But there was one religion, warmly acknowledged wherever the system of caste existed; the worship of "the Almighty Rupee." Men whose neglect of ritual observances had led to their excommunication were heavily fined on re-admission to the intercourse of their respective brotherhoods: and an all-powerful Government could always expose its troops to these penalties. More than a generation had elapsed since a sort of passive mutiny due to that cause had been violently extinguished and quenched in blood at Barrackpore: yet the Government had continued to tamper with the caste-rules of their native soldiery, and, by so doing, to render them liable to social penalties. Again, the religion of the rupee had been attacked in another way by recent reforms of the pension-establishment; stringent rules having been issued for the guidance of invaliding committees whereby the pensions that the sepoys had been accustomed to consider secured to length of service were withheld until the applicant could produce a medical certificate of not being able to stand up under his arms. This might relieve the pension-list, but could it have a good effect either on those in the service or on their friends outside? Then there was the annexation of Oude, the home of so many of the sepoys; whereby not only was a shock given to the public conscience but also to the prestige of the native soldier. The profligacy and maladministration of the Court of Oude might be distressing to ideas of official purity derived from a different form of civilisation; but people might well ask whether such considerations necessarily led to the exile of a friendly prince and the sequestration of the whole revenues of his principality—a principality which we had ourselves erected into a kingdom. It was felt by others than natives that a less arbitrary and less revolutionary measure might have secured the welfare of the people of Oude. Those among them who were connected with the army were absolutely injured by the annexation; for they lost privileges which they had hitherto enjoyed as servants of the paramount power domiciled in a tributary state.* Nor were these the only causes of discontent: innumerable faults had weakened the military system. The regiments were in a high state of pipe-clay, but they were too much alike. It may be an objection to organising an army in corps of different races and creeds that they will show jealousies and create disturbances when cantoned or brigaded together; but the opposite evil was now seen to be far greater. When (with the sole exception of a few non-Hindustánis in distinct corps, none of which joined the revolt) you had Sikhs, Pathans, and Hindustanis blended together in equal proportions in all corps, the Bengal Infantry resembled a country in which the same strata pervaded the whole structure of the land. A connection of comradeship was substituted for the dissidences of blood and belief; the shock of a convulsion once communicated ran through the whole body in which the new solidarity prevailed. Further, the commandants had lost their free scope of action, and with it their hold over their men; centralisation had brought its procrustean uniformity, its dead-level of mechanical mediocrity. A battalion's appearance in peace was taken as a sign of its efficiency for war; the colonel was saved the trouble of originality by a code of the minutest regulations; corporal punishment was abolished for the sepoys, though they were paraded to see their white comrades flogged; the sentence of a regimental court-martial was liable to probable reversal on appeal or reference; the younger English officers were sometimes spoken of as "the refuse," when they were really disappointed men, rotting in undesired idleness, because they had nothing to do in their regiments, and wanted the interest requisite to the obtaining of staff-employ.† That they

* It should be noted that in Oude—though in Oude only—the rising was both national and universal, and inspired by a really patriot spirit.

† It should here be noted that Haileybury students who failed to qualify for the Civil Service, were usually sent out to India as military officers.

were not intrinsically bad material, may be inferred from the good service performed by their contemporaries who obtained civil preferment or were attached to the staff of the army, and from the universal courage and confidence in their men that they themselves showed at a time when confidence had ceased to be well-founded or courage to be of use. But that could not be a good system which taught a young man, on entering the ranks of the army, to make it his constant object to get away from them, and which led him to regard his regiment as a place of punishment,* and to look upon his native comrades as the instruments of his torture; while, in the meantime, the fortunate emancipated ones were kept free from military duties till they almost changed their nature, and then, on promotion, returned to their corps, which they were to manage without power, and lead without experience.

Given these conditions, can we wonder at the result? They may be thus summarised:—

1st. A body of pampered mercenaries, over-disciplined, wrongly enregimented, threatened in their caste, their privileges, their pensions.

2nd. Inefficiency of regimental officers, combined with a starved military administration. For example, the means of transport had been abolished for a saving of seventy thousand rupees per annum. The consequence was seen when it took the head-quarters a month to get from Ambála to Dehli after the outbreak in May.

3rd. Weakened confidence in British probity. This affected all classes at the time—some less, some more.

The Native Army, in this state of demoralisation, would form a fit subject for treasonable tampering on the part of friends of the dethroned King of Oude and the threatened family of Dehli. A day fixed for a rising—Mr. Wilson, in his intercourse with the soldiery, learned that the 31st of May had been the day

* Regimental employ was actually so used in the case of officers whose offences were not considered heinous enough to require trial by court-martial.

originally determined; imperfectly concerted plans; action precipitated by injudicious conduct (over-ruled by Britain's fortune to a happy result); such seem sufficient causes to account for the origin of the great rebellion.

Most, if not all, of the evils and dangers above signalised, have now been removed; and the suggestions here made may perhaps seem to deserve to be consigned to the category of post-eventual wisdom. I may, however, add that many civil officers of those days were aware of the unsatisfactory state of things in the Bengal Army; and that the above statements are taken, with but trifling alterations, from a letter which the present writer addressed to a friend in England on the 6th June 1857. His excuse for reproducing them here is that, so far as he is informed, the truths that they may contain ought never to be lost sight of nor forgotten. The love of uniformity and paper-symmetry will never be banished from the average official mind. All sorts of financial mirage will always tempt rulers thirsting for money to make a show with. But the great need of public life, without which the devotion of civil administrators loses half its effect, will always be—in one word—Discipline. And this is the one thing that the average official mind is too prone to sacrifice.

Let a final remark be permitted as to the effect of that much-debated institution, the system, so-called, of Caste :—

Among other difficulties attending the scheme, if such there was, for taking advantage of the temporary weakness of Government to promote a general rising of the country, must be noticed the extraordinary absence of solidarity in a land peopled, like India, by discordant tribes. What is generally known as "the system of caste" must, no doubt, have the effect of hampering any united effort for national independence. Indeed, a vast region so inhabited can hardly be called "a country," so as to be conceived of as animated by a spirit of common patriotism. What takes that form in other parts of the world, will be here split up and represented by a hundred or a thousand displays of what the natives call "brotherhood." That spirit, arising out of the archaic Aryan institution of the Corporate Family, causes the members of each tribe to feel as if they were all of kin, and will also lead to a feeling of smouldering but real hostility against every other tribe, and thus prevent effective combination. In this respect the British in India have an advantage over the French in Algeria, and over the Russians in Central Asia.

On the other hand, it must be allowed that this spirit sometimes acted unfavourably on the efforts of the Government to maintain order. The native officials often tried to do their duty. But they could not combine for administrative purposes as did their British colleagues. This has been lately pointed out by an intelligent writer who has been contributing some papers to the *Pioneer*, an excellent local journal. It is conclusively shown in all the *Narratives* from which our story has been gathered that "A. P. W."—whether or no he was present at the time—is quite justified in his description of the difficulties encountered by those native officials who remained faithful.

On the whole, therefore, and without any conscious yielding to Chauvinist bias, it will be probably admitted that the presence of one or two well-selected English officers in every county of British India was an absolute advantage to the cause of order, next only in value—if in any degree subordinate—to the presence of loyal and trustworthy bodies of troops. It would have been of little avail to kill or expel the mutinous sepoys, or to burn down the hovels of rebellious villagers, if there had not been intelligent, humane, impartial agents at hand to encourage the well-affected and heal the ravages of fire and sword. At the same time it is equally plain that, when once rebellion had broken out, the best efforts of civil officers would have been of little avail without the gallant concurrence of the soldiers and their brave leaders. If India was saved, it was *tam Marte quam Mercurio*, the exploit of the "United Service."

APPENDIX.—P. 110 ff.

The sentence "On the 20th August the Gurkhas arrived under Colonel Wroughton, followed on the 3rd," &c., &c. *should be read as follows*:—

"On or about the 26th August the Gurkhas arrived under Colonel Wroughton, accompanied by Mr. W. Wynyard, C.S., his subordinate, Mr. Bird, remaining for the time (against advice), at Gorakhpur, whence he escaped, ultimately, to Ballia."

And for "Mr. Bird soon after took another party," *should be read*:—

"Mr. Wynyard soon after took out a party consisting of a wing H. M. 10th Foot, with some Gurkhas and Bengal Artillery," &c.

The Author regrets that these corrections—which are from good authority—did not reach him in time to be embodied in the text.